TWAYNE'S WORLD AUTHORS SERIES

A Survey of the World's Literature

Sylvia E. Bowman, Indiana University

GENERAL EDITOR

SPAIN

Gerald E. Wade, Vanderbilt University

Janet Winecoff Díaz, University of North Carolina

EDITORS

Antonio de Guevara

TWAS 360

Antonio de Guevara

By JOSEPH R. JONES

University of Kentucky

TWAYNE PUBLISHERS

A DIVISION OF G. K. HALL & CO., BOSTON

Library of Congress Cataloging in Publication Data

Jones, Joseph Ramon, 1935–
    Antonio de Guevara.

    (Twayne's world authors series; TWAS 360: Spain)
    Bibliography: pp. 165–72
    Includes index.
    1. Guevara, Antonio de, Bp., d. 1545?
PQ6398.G9J6   868'.3'09   75–4572
ISBN 0–8057–2409–5

MANUFACTURED IN THE UNITED STATES OF AMERICA

FOR MARGARET

Contents

About the Author

Joseph R. Jones, a Texan educated at Sewanee and Wisconsin, has been a member of the faculty of the University of Kentucky since 1967. He had previously taught at the University of North Carolina. His academic credentials include fellowships at Wisconsin, Mexico City College and San Marcos in Lima. Dr. Jones has published studies on comparative literature, folklore, and emblem literature as well as on writers of the Spanish Renaissance, including Nebrija, Montemayor, Avellaneda, López de Ubeda and Gracián. Among his studies on Guevara are an essay on the famous bishop's lost notebooks and an edition of his lives of ten Roman emperors (*Una década de Césares*).

Preface

I have written this book in the belief that the idea behind the Twayne World Authors Series is a sound one: that a serious but nontechnical survey of the life and works of important foreign (as well as English) authors fills a gap in the material available to cultured English-speaking readers, who may not have the linguistic or the bibliographical expertise to find a general work. In the case of Guevara, with the exception of Ernest Grey's new study, there is no work in English on this extremely important writer. The present book aspires to be a modest digest of Bishop Guevara's life, his books, and the scholarship devoted to them.

I have leaned very heavily on preceding *guevaristas*, without whom this book would have, literally, been impossible to write. I must make special mention of René Costes, killed in the First World War before his books on Guevara could be published; J. Gibbs, whose excellent biography and articles on Guevara have provided basic material; Ernest Grey, friend and collaborator on a forthcoming edition of the *Relox de príncipes*, and whose *Guevara, A Forgotten Rennaisance Author* (The Hague: Nijhoff, 1973) is the first English study of Guevara; María Rosa Lida de Malkiel, whose infuriating bias against Guevara has made me think hard before taking a stand on any issue in Guevara scholarship; and Francisco Márquez Villanueva, the most interesting modern critic of Guevara. These authors have affected my attitude as much as anything, though I may actually owe more data to such students as Fr. Angel Uribe and Fr. Fidèle de Ros. And it was a *guevarista* who never published, my mentor at the University of Wisconsin, J. Homer Herriott, a man who through years of meticulous scholarship had trained his eye and ear to the vanished beauties of classical rhetoric, that first made me see the elegance of Guevara's style, his wit, and his influence on subsequent Spanish genres or writers; so I must include him in my list of acknowledgments. Finally, I must add that this book would have been a far better one had not Ernest Grey died before he could see the manuscript.

After some years of reading sixteenth-century Spanish and English, I find that the Spanish (a very conservative language compared with ours) is still much more accessible than the now antiquated English of the sixteenth-century versions; thus, I have translated all the quotations into plain modern idiom instead of using the quaint language of, say, North. I consider my translations accurate, but I have not scrupled to tighten the free syntax (which was perfectly acceptable in Guevara's day) or to make reasonable substitutions of vocabulary where I thought it would help recreate the rhetorical effect of the prose. A translator must work to please himself, since he can be sure that any moderately competent reader of Spanish will quibble with his rendition.

I would like also to thank the Kentucky Research Foundation for typing funds; to reiterate my gratitude to Mrs. Celinda Todd, the typist, whose skill in deciphering my rough draft was a source of constant amazement; and to acknowledge my debt to Gerald E. Wade for his patience and editorial wisdom.

JOSEPH R. JONES

The University of Kentucky, Lexington

Chronology

1535   Guevara accompanies Charles on the military expedition to Tunis; the bishop has charge of the field hospital.

1537   Guevara becomes bishop of Mondoñedo, in Galicia.

1539   Guevara publishes *The Lives of Ten Emperors, A Dispraise of the Life of a Courtier, The Favored Courtier, The Art of Navigation,* and the first volume of his *Familiar Letters.*

1541   Guevara publishes the *Second Part* of his letters.

1542   Guevara publishes his *Monks' Chapel.*

1545   Guevara publishes part one of *The Mount of Calvary,* the second part of which appears posthumously in 1549. On April 3, Bishop Antonio de Guevara dies in Mondoñedo. The Council of Trent begins.

CHAPTER 1

Guevara's Life

THE life of Antonio de Guevara "spans the greater part of the reigns of the Catholic Monarchs, Joan the Mad, and Charles V. In the sixty-four years of his life, from 1481 to his death in 1545, Spain finished the Reconquest, Columbus discovered the New World, the government imposed religious uniformity, Valencia and Castile went through civil wars, Spanish troops completed the domination of Italy, conquered Tunisia, and stopped the advance of Francis I, and Spain became the great power of Europe. Guevara was present as an eyewitness at some of these events; his relatives took part in others. In half a century he saw a divided country rise to become a worldwide empire, and within the limits of his own abilities, he himself played a part in this rapid development." Thus J. Gibbs, in the opening pages of his biography of Guevara—on which this account will principally be based—characterizes the background against which the literary and social activities of Guevara must be seen in order to be evaluated properly.[1] Fray Antonio and his brother, Dr. Fernando de Guevara, are extraordinary examples of an emerging social type which develops as the new state evolves; they are men from old families who advance by their talents and services to the state, in competition with the anachronistic *conquistadores* of the New World, the fabulously wealthy *indianos* ("rich Americans"), bankers, and merchants, and the throngs of talented aspirants from lower social categories. Fray Antonio is the more famous of the two brothers for the remarkable success of his writings; Fernando was the more practical and influential in his own day.[2] But both of them have affected the development of the modern world: Antonio, through the virtually incalculable influence of his prose, Fernando through his participation in some of the most dramatic decisions of state during the sixteenth century.

13

The Guevaras were *montañeses*, that is, natives of north-central Spain, a section of the country proverbial for the purity of its blood and the valor of its aristocracy. The family rose to moderate prominence in the early fifteenth century, during the reign of John II (Don Beltrán de Guevara, fray Antonio's grandfather, was made count of Tahalú in 1417) but suffered from financial difficulties in fray Antonio's day.[3]

With regard to fray Antonio's immediate family, there is some uncertainty (as there is about many points of his biography, such as his birthday and birthplace), which arises from the discrepancies among fray Antonio's own offhanded remarks about his parentage, a mid-seventeenth-century genealogy, and the pedigree filed by his brother Fernando upon his entry into the order of the knights of St. James. Since at present these inconsistencies are unresolved, it seems best to accept fray Antonio's own version of his family tree, with one important qualification based on Fernando's pedigree: the father of both Antonio and Fernando was Juan Beltrán de Guevara, though fray Antonio always calls him Beltrán. According to the seventeenth-century family history, this Juan Beltrán de Guevara was one of six illegitimate children of Count Beltrán.[4]

The year 1481, usually given as Antonio's birthdate, is open to question. From his own remarks, it is possible to deduce three dates, ranging from 1474 to 1480, but on the basis of a now destroyed document from the monastery where Guevara professed, it appears that he was born in 1481. His birthplace was probably the village of Treceño, a town where he passed at least part of his childhood, according to a line in one of his letters. He himself tells us very little about his youth: "When I was twelve years old, my father brought me to court... where I was educated, grew, and lived for some time."[5] At least two of his relatives were court functionaries, his uncle Ladrón de Guevara, the queen's chamberlain, and another uncle, Iñigo, Prince John's carver. Prince John (the son of Ferdinand and Isabel) died in 1497, don Ladrón de Guevara in 1503, and Queen Isabel in 1504; if Antonio were still living at court under the patronage of his relatives—a possibility unsubstantiated by any evidence—then the dissolution of the two royal households, as well as his uncle's death, would surely have affected his position. All he tells us, however, is that, "since Prince John had died and Queen Isabel passed away, it pleased our Lord to take me out of the vices of the world and make me a Franciscan monk" (*Menosprecio*, p. 10).

Antonio entered the Franciscan order in Valladolid in 1505. From his letters, prefaces, and from the lost document on which his birth date is based, we learn that he held various responsible positions in the order: he was guardian of the monasteries of Arévalo, Avila, and Soria (to which he left money in his will, "because I have scruples about the time that I administered the aforesaid monastery"),[6] custos of the province of La Concepción, and definitor of the order, by election, in 1520. During the fifteen years between Antonio's profession and the beginning of the civil war known in Castile as the rebellion of the communes (*comunidades*), Philip of Burgundy and Joan the Mad ruled briefly; Ferdinand the Catholic retired to Aragon and then once again assumed the rulership of the united kingdoms of Castile and Aragon; and at Ferdinand's death in 1516, Cardinal Cisneros exercised the regency for one year. In 1517, Joan the Mad's eldest son, Charles, a homely, French-speaking youth who had never been to Spain, arrived with a crowd of rapacious Flemings and remained only a short three years before leaving for Germany, where he literally bought the Imperial crown for himself.

Charles's Spanish subjects were unhappy with their young king's ambition to follow his paternal grandfather as ruler of the Holy Roman Empire, though they might have overlooked his neglect of them if he had been more careful of Spanish sensitivity. But when he appointed Adrian of Utrecht (the future Pope Adrian VI) to remain behind as regent, he committed a serious *faux pas*. The delegation of such authority to a foreigner was intolerable, and, beginning with Toledo, Castilian cities repudiated the authority of the regent. Adrian ordered the burning of Medina del Campo, Castile's great trade center, and thereby alienated still more loyal subjects. Fifteen cities formed a league against the regent, though Charles soon managed to convert most of the nobility and clergy to the royalist side again by appointing two Spaniards to share the regency. The common people, however, were by this time demanding "unnatural" privileges and were unwilling to submit to the new regency. In April of

1521, a royalist army defeated the forces of the communes, and the Castilian rebellion ended.

Antonio was an eyewitness of many of the important moments of the rebellion, and he appears to owe his return to court, as preacher of the royal chapel, at least in part, to his activities on the side of the royalists.[7] But his own indifference to exact detail in reporting these events, particularly dates, and his tendency to distort historical material in order to enhance its moral import have made it almost impossible to untangle the factual from the fictional. Opinions differ radically over how much of his own account may be accepted. Henry Seaver, author of the standard work on the communes, rejects Guevara's claims altogether.[8] Paul Merimée believes that Guevara probably worked with some of the important mediators and then years later tended to exaggerate his part.[9]

In late 1521, the regents, in the name of the king, wrote to fray Antonio asking him to come to court as preacher of the royal chapel. He undertook the new duties in 1523. Documents are scanty, but Gibbs is doubtless correct when he assumes that the friar followed the movements of the court in these years (1521–25) for which there exists little information.

Coincident in time with the commune rebellion in Castile is the war of the brotherhoods (*germanías*) in Valencia, in which ultimately the nobility and common people were again pitted against each other, though for entirely different reasons. The large remnant of Moorish peasants in Valencia supplied labor and taxes for the nobility, who therefore viewed their religious practices with indulgence. The common people, however, envied the prosperity of the Moriscos and accused them of collusion with the pirates who constantly raided the coast. In 1519, a Valencian mob rioted over an incident of no political significance and refused to disband a "brotherhood" which it organized for self-defense. Charles, leaving hastily for Germany, confirmed its right to organize and thereby offended the nobles and parliament; but when the brotherhood became difficult to control, the regent and eventually the disaffected nobles banded together to defeat the movement. The real victims of the rebellion were the Moorish vassals who were either slaughtered by the rebels or forcibly

baptized in huge numbers, thus bringing them under the juris-
diction of the Inquisition.

The newly made Christians, with little understanding of their
official religion, often with no knowledge of Spanish, naturally
continued to practice their old religion outside the mosques-
turned-into-churches. In 1525, the emperor convened a group of
distinguished theologians and statesmen in Madrid for the purpose of considering the religious aspects of the Moorish question.
Fray Antonio and his brother were among this group, fray Antonio being the only person not a prelate or member of one of
the royal councils.[10] The group decided, in the face of ample
evidence to the contrary, that no force or violence had been used
on the Moriscos and that as a result, they should be compelled
to fulfill obligations of their new faith. Four commissioners were
then sent to Valencia to inspire a more fervent Christianity among
the apostate and to take legal action against the refractory. Guevara was one of the four chosen. His success, after three months
of efforts, is attested by a laudatory letter from the emperor
and by subsequent events. The satisfactory results obtained by
the commissioners stimulated the emperor to decree in the fall
of 1525, as an act of gratitude for the victory over Francis I at
Pavia, the conversion of all those Moriscos who had escaped the
germanías; the alternative was emigration under difficult circumstances.

Guevara headed the three commissioners appointed for this
new task and himself promulgated the emperor's edict from the
pulpit of the cathedral of Valencia in October of 1525. He
preached a sermon in which he emphasized the part-Christian
ancestry of the Valencian Moorish population, using this clever
approach to attract the unconverted. For two months the commissioners worked to convert the Moriscos, against stubborn re-
sistance on the part of the proselytes and their Christian lords.
Someone, however, suggested an effective solution for reconciling
the intransigent emperor and the equally stiff-necked Moriscos:
the latter chose twelve *alfaquíes* ("magistrates") to interview
the emperor, ascertain exactly how committed he was to the
conversion, and bargain for concessions. Fr. Angel Uribe, who
presents abundant evidence for the case, believes that Guevara
conceived this scheme. In any event, it was Guevara who accom-

panied the magistrates to and from court and was charged with promulgating the capitulations; these were so acceptable that the *alfaquíes* and their followers submitted to baptism without further delay. In a letter to the commissioners, referring to fray Antonio, the inquisitor general praises him, observing that "his arrival and the coming of the aforesaid representatives have certainly been fruitful in this holy business, which, praised be God, progresses better and better. . . ." Uribe concludes that "it is logical therefore to attribute to him the double merit of having managed to rechannel the complex Morisco problem and of having been one of its principal agents" (240–41). With the reduction of two armed camps of Moriscos who had refused to surrender to the emperor's commands (1520), Guevara's tasks in Valencia were finished.

In the summer of 1526, fray Antonio joined the court, which had moved into the Alhambra, in Granada, where the emperor and his new bride, Isabel of Portugal, were spending their honeymoon. Shortly after the emperor's arrival, his Morisco vassals presented a formal complaint of the oppressive treatment they suffered from the Christian settlers who had been flowing into the kingdom since its conquest in 1492. The favorable conditions of the original treaty of surrender had been forgotten, and ever harsher measures had failed to integrate the Morisco element into Spanish Christian society. The Moriscos had also used bribery to soften the terms of new edicts and were understandably skeptical of the emperor's apparent determination to eradicate apostasy. The Morisco petition was answered by a Christian complaint against the subversive activities of Morisco subjects. The emperor turned the documents over to the Council of State, which in turn appointed five examiners (*visitadores*) to visit the kingdom and investigate the complaints of both sides. Antonio was obviously an expert in such affairs and was named as one of the *visitadores*. The problem, summed up by Guevara, was that the Moriscos had been too poorly instructed in matters of the faith and the king's justices had winked at their activities for too long. The findings of the examiners were that apostasy was widespread and the complaints of the Moriscos unjustified. The emperor convened another meeting of theologians, including Father Guevara, and issued a list of stringent new regulations, although he soon suspended them out of consideration of a Morisco gift of eighty thousand ducats.

Toward the end of 1526, Guevara was appointed official chronicler as successor of Peter Martyr, a distinguished Italian humanist who is best known for his *Decades de Orbe Novo*, on the discovery of America. Guevara received regular payment as chronicler from 1527 until the year before his death, although he tells us in his first will that he ceased work on the history after 1537.[11]

In the summer of 1527, the inquisitor general called a meeting of twenty-nine distinguished churchmen, among them the increasingly important friar, and charged them with an examination of passages in Erasmus's works which were considered heretical by his opponents.[12] Fray Antonio's autograph opinions, preserved in the Inquisition's archives, are uniformly unfavorable and range from a total condemnation of the *Colloquia* as "depraved" to mild disapproval of certain "improper locutions."[13]

In 1528, Guevara saw a concrete result of his diligent service to the crown in religious matters—proof that the emperor's letter of commendation of 1525 (after Guevara's missionary work among Valencian Moriscos), which concludes "I shall not forget your good services," was not mere rhetoric. Guevara was named bishop of Guadix, a small diocese near Granada.

Whatever Guevara's literary reputation may have been up to the year 1528, it was to take a new course with the appearance in print of three unauthorized editions of his historical novel, *The Golden Book of Marcus Aurelius* (*Libro áureo de Marco Aurelio*), at Lisbon, Seville, and Valencia. Guevara had been working on this remarkable book since 1518, according to his own account, and had presented the manuscript of it to the emperor for his private amusement. The manuscript, copied and passed around among the courtiers, had found its way to the hands of unscrupulous printers. Manuscripts, even when widely circulated, were not subject to the same restrictions as printed materials, and Guevara must have felt free to invent not only edifying details of the Roman emperor's life, but such original touches as love letters and an exchange of insults with a group of Roman whores. The appearance of the pirated editions was a mixed blessing, however.[14] Undoubtedly the amorous pas-

sages, bland though they now seem, and the "pagan" tone of
the book were an embarrassment to a prominent churchman
whose publications should have been wholly exemplary and
Christian. In order to counteract the bad impression, Guevara
reworked *The Golden Book* and issued it the following year with
a new title, *The Dial of Princes* (*Relox de príncipes*), and a long
preface disclaiming responsibility for its premature publication.
The two works, *The Golden Book* and *The Dial*, both of which
were reprinted many times, made Guevara the most famous
Spanish author of his day. The very learned may have considered
fray Antonio's works appalling forgeries, but the style, anecdotes,
wit, and high moral tone even of *The Golden Book*, made them
best-sellers at a time when there was little competition from
other books of their kind in Spain, or, indeed, the rest of Europe.

Guevara, occupied with activities at court, inquisitorial duties,
and the chores of book publishing, did not go to his new diocese
until the fall of 1529, where he apparently remained until 1531.
During the new bishop's tenure, two litigations occupied his
mind. Out of context, they seem petty, strident, and unworthy of
the high-born litigants. But such squabbles were apparently common, and Guevara's fulminations and threats are consistent with
his temperament and with a legitimate desire to place Spain's
poorest diocese on a sounder financial basis.

Guevara's skill as a preacher had brought him to court or at
least influenced his assignment to the royal chapel. The earliest
datable example of his oratory, however, is not a sermon but
a speech delivered in Madrid in September of 1528—by the
emperor. "The composition of this discourse belongs, without
doubt, to Charles V's preacher, the famous fray Antonio de
Guevara, recently created bishop of Guadix, who at that time
accompanied the emperor by reason of his double office as
preacher of the royal chapel and imperial chronicler." In announcing his departure for Italy with the intentions of being
crowned by the pope and of persuading the pope to convoke a
general council, Charles emphasized that his desire was to conserve only what was his by right of inheritance and that he did
not seek to acquire the territory of other monarchs. "These con-
cepts, which are found *ad pedem litterae* in the *Dial of Princes*,"
were contrary to the policies of the Italian chancellor Mercurio di

Gattinara, who favored conquest; such an idea was repudiated with scorn by the emperor, adopting Guevara's phrases. "And this occurred not only on the occasion of the solemn discourse but it was a fixed norm of conduct for the emperor, who perhaps inspired, in turn, the doctrine of the *Dial of Princes*."[15]

The bishop appears to have led a private life in the six years following the publication of the *Dial of Princes* (1529), but in 1535, he took part in an expedition of international importance, the campaign against Turkish pirates in Tunisia.

By the 1530s, the Turkish empire under Suleiman had become a serious threat to the Holy Roman Empire and to the Mediterranean coastal cities. The efforts of Andrea Doria to restrain Turkish piracy were insufficient to stop the equally brilliant Redbeard, corsair and commander-in-chief of the Turkish fleet. In 1534, Redbeard captured Tunis and made himself king. This action spurred Charles, who had gained the support of the Genoese, to concentrate on the Turkish problem in the western Mediterranean; and after complicated diplomatic maneuvers and extensive preparations, he readied himself to lead in person an expedition against the strongholds of Redbeard in Tunisia. One can still feel the excitement and glamour of this expedition in the contemporary accounts. It was a kind of new crusade, led by the champion of Christianity against the Turkish infidels' great admiral, and it would have important spiritual as well as worldly advantages if successfully concluded.

On May 30, 1535, the fleet sailed out of Barcelona for Mallorca, Sardinia, and North Africa. The cream of Spanish and Portuguese nobility accompanied the emperor, along with many important foreigners, each with his servants, horses, and equipment. Aside from Spanish and foreign soldiers in the pay of the emperor, other people without pay—adventurers, gentlemen, men of means, tradesmen, merchants, monks, and clerks—crowded into the boats, along with four thousand ladies of easy virtue, who were ejected from some boats by order of the council of war, only to be received by the others.

By June 18, the imperial forces were skirmishing with the Turks near the fortress of La Goleta, and fray Antonio began "with a will and much charity" to supervise the care of the wounded. Another chronicler tells us that the bishop had four chaplains and 250 beds at his disposal.[16] La Goleta was not taken until July 14, and beneath the spectacular, chivalrous veneer of the chronicles, the disagreeable realities of war began to tell: sickness, diminishing provisions, the stench of dead bodies, the emperor's ailments.

Redbeard slipped out of the fortress of Tunis, and the imperial forces entered it on July 21, freeing over sixteen thousand captives. Andrea Doria pursued Redbeard to the city of Bona, near the ancient site of Hippo, but the wily corsair escaped. The emperor signed a treaty which reinstated the former king of Tunisia and departed for Sicily and Naples, parts of his maternal inheritance which he had never seen. The emperor then moved on to Rome, where he spent Holy Week of 1536 amid the rich and splendid ceremonies of the papal court. He attended mass dressed after the fashion of the ancient Caesars and, as the pope's temporal counterpart, he imitated the pontifical ceremonies, standing and sitting when the pope did, removing his crown when the pope removed his tiara. He also visited the tourist sights of Rome in disguise.

The mounting difficulties with France, revived by the death of the duke of Milan, embittered the emperor's stay in Rome. The French ambassador circulated slanders which so annoyed Charles that he persuaded the pope to assemble the diplomatic corps, the college of Cardinals, and a large crowd of important people so that he could make a public reply. The oration is almost certainly the work of Guevara: "either Charles the Fifth had entirely assimilated the style of his preacher (which is scarcely possible) or this speech, like the two earlier ones, is Guevara's."[17]

The speech, in Spanish, reviewed the history of the rivalry between the houses of Austria and France, accused Francis I of perjury, of ingratitude for the clemency of his captors, of aiding the Turkish enemies of Christ, etc., and it publicly challenged Francis to a duel. The pope was so enthusiastic that he interrupted the speech to embrace and kiss Charles and then tried to calm his anger. The French ambassador, who did not understand Spanish, requested a copy to send to Francis, and the emperor (whose native language was of course French) was delighted to repeat it to him.

Hostilities between France and the emperor broke out again

in 1536, and the emperor himself headed the campaign in southern France. After two years of inconclusive fighting, a ten-year truce was arranged, and the emperor returned to Spain from Italy, into which he had withdrawn from Provence.

Guevara apparently accompanied the imperial household in its travels from North Africa. He himself gives us little information. He tells us that he held debates with Jews in Naples and Rome and that he made no conversions. His reaction to Rome is typically Guevarian. One would expect a man whose best-known works are recreations of Rome's imperial days to show a great interest in her monuments and history; yet almost his only references are to her immorality. In any event, Guevara left the imperial party in Genoa and took passage for Barcelona in late 1536.

On the return journey from the expedition to Tunisia, Charles promoted a number of courtiers, among them Guevara, whom he nominated for appointment to the see of Mondoñedo. The list of candidates for various positions still exists, and beside Guevara's name, the emperor himself wrote "nominate." (Gibbs has discovered in an earlier list a curious note beside Guevara's name: "increase salary by two hundred ducats, for good work." The note was then crossed out by another hand [*Vida*, pp. 49–50].) Guevara's name was presented to the pope in late 1536, and he was promoted in April, 1537.[18]

The Galician diocese of Mondoñedo, though relatively poor, had a greater income than Guadix, and the bishop received an increase of 750 ducats per annum. The fees involved in such nominations were large, however, and Guevara had to borrow money from his brother-in-law to pay for the papal bull. Guevara took possession of the diocese in March of 1538.[19] The rest of his episcopacy is a series of journeys between Mondoñedo, the court, and the Franciscan house in Valladolid, the monastery where he professed and where he died.

Ten years after the appearance of the *Dial of Princes*, the bishop published five books. He had apparently been working on them since 1536, after his return from the Tunisian expedition, because in his first will, he says that he left off writing the imperial chronicle in order to devote his time to "other works." These other works are *The Lives of Ten Emperors, The Favored*

*Courtier, A Dispraise of the Life of a Courtier, The Invention of
the Art of Navigation,* and the *Familiar Letters.*

The *Lives of Ten Emperors,* a book of pagan biography heavily
spiced with fiction, is similar to the first part of *The Golden Book*
in its ethical portraits of ten emperors, beginning with the
Spanish-born Trajan. *The Favored Courtier* and *A Dispraise of
the Life of a Courtier* are closely related. The first is a sort of
guide to success at court, for "privy" courtiers (*privados*) as
well as ordinary courtiers; the second is a detailed account of
the pitfalls of court life and the relative moral safety of life away
from the capital, plus a confession. *The Art of Navigation* is a
very amusing mock-sermon on the discomforts of sea travel, a
by-product of the journey to North Africa and Italy with Charles's
fleet. And the *Familiar Letters* range from sermons to fictional
missives from Plutarch. Of these works, *A Dispraise of the Life
of a Courtier* has had an international success only less than that
of *The Golden Book,* and its influence on Spanish literature is
still being evaluated. The letters were also widely read and
translated, though not everyone liked them: Montaigne, whose
father had them in his library, caustically observed that whoever
had renamed them *The Golden Epistles,* a title under which they
appeared in English, French, Italian, Latin, etc., "had a very
different opinion of them than I have" (*Essais,* I, 48).

After only three years of literary silence, in 1542, Guevara published the *Oratorio de religiosos y ejercicio de virtuosos* (The
Monks' Chapel and Spiritual Exercises for the Virtuous), never
translated into English. In 1545, the year of his death, he issued
The Mount of Calvary, Part I (*Libro llamado Monte Calvario*).
These works contain warmed-over material from his other books,
some out-and-out plagiarism (a common if not approved practice), and sermons, as well as new material.

Part II of *The Mount of Calvary,* which Guevara never finished,
was published posthumously in 1549.

Early in 1544, fray Antonio made a will which is interesting
for the light that it throws on his religious, literary, and personal
activities. It also contributes various details of biography that
are unavailable elsewhere.[20]

Guevara had already constructed a chapel for his remains at
the Franciscan monastery in Valladolid. His brother (the princi-

pal heir) is requested to see that the chapel is paid twelve ducats a year for the celebration of twelve feasts indicated by the bishop, that the silver ornaments are made, that the sculptor is paid, and that a certain person is paid for the marble from which the tombstone was made.

On April 3, 1545, fray Antonio de Guevara expired in his cathedral city of Mondoñedo. According to the provision of his will, he was buried in Mondoñedo, then in 1552, "when our flesh has decayed," the bones were taken to his monastery in Valladolid and interred under the porphyry slab which the bishop had ordered. The chapel, as later described, was a small, dark affair, with one window, an Entombment of Christ over the altar and— at one time, to judge by the second will—twelve polychromed images. The slab which covered the bones of Guevara and his brother contained a Latin poem, and on the wall there was a commemorative slab probably composed by Guevara himself: "In the reign of Charles V, King of Spain, the illustrious friar don Antonio de Guevara, of the province of Alava, the family of Guevara, the order of St. Francis, the habit of this monastery; a theologian by profession, preacher by office; chronicler of the emperor and bishop of Mondoñedo, built [this chapel], A.D. 1542. I have put an end to cares. Farewell hope and fortune." The epitaph reads: "Behold Guevara, saintly priest, famous throughout the world, distinguished in the arts, faithful in religion; he was an outstanding orator, preacher of celestial wisdom; imperial translator and historian. He who covered his lineage with [coarse Franciscan] cloth and who exalted the cloth with a miter is now covered with white marble" (Gibbs, *Vida*, p. 55).

The monastery of St. Francis disappeared in the nineteenth century, and Guevara's bones, now mixed with dust, are not covered *niveo marmore* but by a cinema. Such a transformation is not devoid of mystery, as the moralists of the sixteenth century would have said. It is perfectly symbolic of the triumph of middle-class culture, the decline of the church, and the unrelenting effects of time.

May God rest Guevara's soul. He achieved fame and position in a period of shocking change, when the Reformation had torn up the spiritual unity of Europe, when Charles's spreading empire had raised excruciating questions of the rights of conquest in

America and the justice of suppression of dissent. He is a puzzling mixture of prejudice, kindness, snobbery, humility, fraud, cunning, patriotism, and piety. In short, he is a good example of humanity, fascinating in his contradictory nature, perhaps pitiable because of his inability to resolve his contradictions, and important because he hit upon a literary style which flourished briefly and contributed in no small measure to the currents of thought and expression which flow to us from the sixteenth century, the real source of the modern world.

CHAPTER 2

The Golden Book of Marcus Aurelius

THE first of Guevara's books (which I shall take up in chronological order—so far as it is known—in the following chapters) required the longest period of gestation of all his works,
if one may believe his statement that he worked on it from 1518
until its authorized publication in 1529. Portions of this historical
novel had circulated in manuscript for several years, apparently,
and, as noted above, it appeared in print in 1528, without its
author's permission or name.

I *Contents*

Guevara's masterpiece is the fictionalized biography of a
virtuous pagan emperor, given out as a compilation of hitherto
unknown data from newly discovered manuscripts. It begins
with a long prologue to the Emperor Charles V, "concerning
the translation which he made from Greek into Latin and from
Latin into Spanish, of the book called *The Golden Book*, which
tells of the times of Marcus Aurelius, seventeenth emperor of
Rome." Trying to induce Charles to read this educational and
interesting "translation," Guevara becomes so entangled in his
effort to express frank moral advice with the delicacy due to his
exalted reader that the logic of the resulting prose is often hard
to follow. The gist of most of the prologue is that the desire for
fame—though vain and not really worthy of a Christian—is perfectly human and inevitable; that the emperor, if above ordinary
human concerns, is nevertheless tainted with human foibles;
that he is, in fact, obviously willing to gamble everything for
worldly fame; that what he desires is the good fame deserved
by the virtuous rulers of the past, and that he should therefore
imitate these virtuous rulers. Guevara enumerates the most

illustrious monarchs of antiquity and indicates which virtue was most outstanding in each: legal knowledge in Lycurgus, clemency in Julius Caesar, generosity in Alexander, justice in Trajan, "and finally our present subject, Marcus Aurelius, [famous] because he knew more than all the rest and was friendly with wise men" (12).[1] "It has been my intention, Serene Highness, to persuade you to imitate and follow, not all, not many, not few, but one—Marcus Aurelius alone, whose virtues few or none have equaled" (13).

Guevara is at pains to explain why he has not set some great Christian emperor as a model for Charles rather than a pagan. "I chose to write for you the life of this man, who was a pagan, instead of one who was a Christian, because though your highness is a Christian, if you are wicked, you will have as much infamy in this world and torment in the next as this pagan had glory in this world" (13–14). "I have read much, but sacred literature aside, I have never been so amazed by anything. While translating this book, I was often astounded to see that Divine Providence put so many things into a pagan's understanding" (14).

The text is prefaced by an Argument added by the "translator," who pointedly identifies himself with "my predecessors, the philosophers," the wise advisers of princes who were as much admired in past ages as they are now disesteemed. The current craze for wealth blinds men to true values: "I have entitled this work *The Golden Book* ... because the virtuous will rejoice as much over the discovery, during their lifetime, of this book, with its profound thoughts, as princes rejoice over the discovery of gold mines in the Indies. I promise to all who possess this book that they will find as much profit for their souls in reading it and seeking out its teachings as their bodies will find harm in crossing the seas in search of the gold of the Indies, though I suspect that henceforth there will be more hearts exiled to the golden Indies than eyes occupied in the reading of this work" (19).

The novel itself begins with an account of Marcus Aurelius's lineage, youth, and education which fills the first four chapters. Marcus's father was a descendant of Numa (the first king of Rome) and his mother a descendant of Camillus, but the historians of antiquity do not record "what the condition, estate, poverty, wealth, favor, or disfavor of the parents of Marcus Aurelius the emperor may have been" (30). Guevara "reconstructs" the life of Marcus's father (who was a praetor according to Julius Capitolinus), on the basis of Marcus's correspondence, and he finds that the father was a respected warrior, who defended the empire from the barbarians while stationed at Rhodes for many years. Guevara, explaining the problems of historiography to his reader, says that he rejects other versions of Marcus's early years because of contradictions among the sources. History preserves the names of his teachers, however, and two of them later wrote biographies of their illustrious pupil. Fortunately, Marcus himself also left a letter to his friend Polión which tells how between the ages of eight and ten he learned to read; from ten to thirteen he studied grammar; from thirteen to seventeen, public speaking; and from seventeen to twenty-two, natural philosophy. He then lived on Rhodes ten years reading oratory, after which he moved to Naples to study Greek with a famous scholar. Not long after this, while leading the emperor's army in Dacia, he took up music. Marcus himself is an illustration of his belief, expressed in another letter to Polión, that "nature is content with very little in all things, except in judgment and understanding, which hunger even amid plenty. And since the understanding is of such condition that, when untrammeled, it strays,... it is necessary to lead it on to exalted matters from the very beginning, before it descends to vulgar things" (37–38).

Guevara pursues the themes of chapters 3 and 4, on education and virtuous example, and makes Marcus's children, their upbringing, and child-rearing in general the subject of the next six chapters. Marcus had two sons and four daughters. The eldest son, Verissimus, who died at the age of sixteen, resembled his father and was his father's favorite. The second son, Commodus, was ill-mannered and dissolute but his mother Faustina's favorite. "Aware, then, that the corrupt inclinations of the youth [Commodus] would not be conducive to the good government of the empire," Marcus carefully selected teachers for him who were renowned for their high morals as well as their learning. Of the fourteen (two for each of the seven arts), he

"cashiered" (to use Lawrence Sterne's phrase)[2] five of them
two months later because they behaved improperly at a birthday party: "... they patted their feet ... rocked in their chairs,
clapped their hands, talked loudly, and laughed too much..."
(45, 47). Marcus impresses the rest of the tutors with the
serious duty of educating the royal heir. He urges them to
instill truthfulness, self-control, and chastity in their young
pupil, and to teach him to avoid gambling and idle amusements:
"His youth will require some recreation; which you will allow
him, provided it is infrequent, that it is first measured by
reason, and that it is taken after noble exercises. I do not give
you my son so that you may amuse him but so that you may
teach him" (56).

Marcus's four daughters were entrusted to sturdy wet-nurses
soon after birth and were brought up without ceremony in small
towns near Rome. At the age of two they went to live with
respectable widows who had been successful as tutors of aristocratic children. Marcus never permitted his daughters to return
to the palace until after they married. He was, in fact, so
"severe" and "harsh" with the princesses that Faustina "did
not dare to visit her daughters except surreptitiously" (61).

Since Guevara accepted the idea that the logical goal of a
woman's education is a suitable marriage, he fills chapters 11
to 13 with Marcus's views on the selection of mates. "He married his daughters to native senators, not foreign kings; to men
who with their virtues founded good lineages, not to those
who descended from high-born Romans.... He did not marry
them to men who presumed on the deeds done by their ances-
tors but to those who shone with the deeds of their own
persons" (62).

The next five chapters return to the emperor himself, his
private life, habits, amusements, and routine, beginning with
praise of his pleasant disposition and relaxed, familiar manner
with everyone. But, as Guevara observes, even virtue has its
rivals. And Marcus equally deserves immortality for his tolerance of persons who worked to do him harm. The senator
Fulvius, for example, who had once aspired to be emperor
himself, continually slandered Marcus, and when Marcus freed
a large number of captives by allowing them to touch his robes,

Fulvius made an ironical remark ("My lord, why do you give yourself to everyone?" [76]) which gave the emperor an excuse to air his views on princely familiarity.

The emperor's daily schedule was a model of economy: seven hours of sleep and one for a midday rest; two hours for meals; one hour each for the business of Europe, Asia, and Africa; two hours for private conversations with family and friends; one hour for special cases (e.g., complaints from the poor or widows). Some time was devoted to reading, writing, the composition of poetry, the study of antiquities, or conversations with learned men. He usually went to bed at nine and woke at four; he read until six and then arose in good spirits. For breakfast he had a few mouthfuls of a special conserve of lavender and two draughts of brandy. Depending on the season, he walked abroad or went to one of the public buildings. Once a week, he walked about Rome in case anyone should wish to speak to him.

But even an emperor must have some privacy. Marcus had a study where he kept his books (in Greek, Latin, Chaldean, and Hebrew) and into which he never allowed anyone to enter. "Since it is natural for women to despise what they have and die for what is prohibited" (83), Faustina begs Marcus to let her into the study. She is pregnant and craves to see what is inside. She is certain that he is keeping another woman there. Marcus explodes with wrath at her wheedling; he reviews all of her defects; then he becomes calmer and tries to explain to her why he will not give in to her whims of pregnancy. The chapters taken up with this domestic squabble (19–21) are among the most famous in the book.

When Marcus is fifty-four, he receives the unexpected news that a force of twenty-two thousand Mauritanian soldiers have landed in Great Britain. Marcus immediately embarks the members of his household, who by custom are always prepared for war; but before they sail, a ship arrives from Great Britain with the equally remarkable news that the Mauritanians have all departed. The hasty preparations for war upset the regulation of the imperial household, and the emperor, "seeing the dissolute behavior of his court and the impudence of the officers of his household . . . decided one day to call them together in secret" (93) and speak to them on the evils of idleness. The harangue, one of the longest in the novel, fills chapters 23–25.

Chapters 26–30 deal with a number of topics. Marcus builds a temple at Palermo to commemorate divine punishment of pirates who kept what was not theirs. He writes to a friend Antigonus, exiled to Palermo with his wife and daughter: Antigonus for urinating on the temple walls, his wife for selling amulets against quartern fever, his daughter for consorting with boys. He leaves Rome for Naples because of a plague portended by various striking omens. While there, recuperating from fevers, he reads constantly. (Marcus—like the humanists of the sixteenth century—loved new books: "we do not mean by *new*, books written in his time, but very old ones which because of their antiquity had lain forgotten" [112].) His doctors warn him of the harmful effects of too much reading, and Marcus counters with a long monologue on the benefits of learning and the disastrous effects of ignorance in rulers.

During this convalescence in Naples, Marcus tells his doctors about his first consulship and a speech made by a peasant from the banks of the Danube who had come to the Senate to present a grievance against an unjust Roman administrator. "His face was small, his lips thick, his eyes deep-set, his hair coarse; he wore no hat, shoes of porcupine hide, a goat's hair tunic, a belt of rushes, and carried a staff of wild olive.... Indeed, when I saw him enter the Senate, I thought that he was some animal in human form; but after I had heard him, I judged him to be one of the gods, if there are gods among men" (119). The peasant excoriates the Romans for their greed, which is so great "that the sea could not protect us with its depths nor the earth make us safe with its caves. But I trust in the just gods that, as you unjustly came to drive us from our homes and land, so others will come who with justice may drive you from Italy and Rome. It is an infallible rule that he who takes by force what is not his, loses his rights to his own property" (119-20).

Why should Rome have invaded Germany? The Germans were not enemies or allies of Rome's enemies; they lived in peace with their neighbors. Rome never sought their friendship and has no hereditary or legal right of possession. To compound her crimes, Rome has sent governors who are ignorant and corrupt, whereas captured territory should be so well ruled that the conquered forget that they are being tyrannized.

According to Marcus, the senators were so ashamed after this speech that they could not answer the peasant. The next day, the Senate had his speech inscribed in a book of famous actions, made him a Roman citizen and pensioner, and arranged to send new judges to Germany.

Faustina asks to have her eldest daughter Lucilla present at an imperial triumph. Marcus agrees, but the unaccustomed freedom goes to Lucilla's head and she behaves very immodestly ("In those days, for a Roman girl to laugh with the men was tantamount to a Greek woman's committing adultery with a priest" [129]). When the celebrations are over, Lucilla and her mother wander about Rome sightseeing and amusing themselves. Marcus scolds them, "not because I think that your daughter is bad but because you give her an opportunity not to be good" (138). Modest, retiring behavior, separation from all men, even relatives, and useful occupation are the proper way to bring up a girl (chs. 34–38).

Marcus's final illness and last speech to his friends and his son occupy chapters 39–48. During a winter campaign, near Vienna, Marcus suffers a stroke. He is depressed, and his secretary upbraids him for not facing death courageously. But Marcus says that his sorrow is not for his imminent death but because he leaves Commodus "at an age dangerous to himself and difficult for the empire" (162). He is not afraid of death, like the enlightened pagan he is, but is joyous at the prospects of release. "Sixty-two years ago Earth created this piece of earth; it is now time for her to acknowledge me as her son and me her as my mother. Certainly she is a kind mother, for though I have trampled her under my feet for so long a time, she now receives me into her bosom forever" (171). He then addresses the prince's tutors, charging them to have only the good of the empire as their goal and to put aside personal envy and hatred.

At dawn the next day, the emperor calls his son, warns him of the pitfalls of rulership (he compares the court to a merchant's stall where people buy and sell lies, reputations, etc.), and gives him a series of principles for good government: to seek

advice, not to allow one person or group too much influence,
to be chary of counsel that harms another, to honor religion
and family, to be compassionate. The emperor's last act is to
give to Commodus a tryptich of ivory and rare woods which
once hung over the bed of the pharaohs. It depicts various gods
and contains a poem which is, in aphoristic form, a summary of
all that Marcus has told his son.

"Here ends the first book, called *The Golden Book*, which
treats of the times of Marcus Aurelius, seventeenth emperor
of Rome; it was translated by the Rev. Fr. Friar Antonio de
Guevara, preacher in the royal chapel of His Sacred Catholic
Caesarean Majesty" (192).

Book Two of *The Golden Book* is a collection of nineteen
letters which, according to the title, "show the subtlety of the
emperor's wit and the profundity of his thought." The variety
of subject matter, even in a single letter, makes it difficult to
summarize these chapters, but broadly speaking, they treat
problems of death (1, 8), avarice (2, 3), the reverses of fortune
(5, 6, 19), injustice (10, 12), war (4), folly in old people (7), and
public morals (11). Love letters (13–18) form an interesting
group apart. They range from a satirical letter to some prosti-
tutes who have lampooned Marcus in a skit to a bitter exchange
between Marcus and an aging ex-mistress.

Within the fiction of the novel they are important for the
rounding out of the characters of Marcus, his family, and his
friends, and they form a sort of appendix of original source
material on which the historical reconstructions of the novel
partially depend.

II *Sources*

"... There have been many who wrote of the times of this
excellent emperor, Marcus Aurelius: to wit, Herodian, who
wrote little, Eutropius, less, Lampridius, much less, and Julius
Capitolinus, somewhat more. The writings of these men and
of others seem more like epitomes than histories. There is
another difference between this work and theirs: they wrote
from hearsay but the writers from whose work I composed the
present one were eyewitnesses, who did not hear what they

wrote about from others but who saw it themselves. Among the teachers who taught this emperor were three (namely, Junius Rusticus, Cinna Catulus, and Sextus Chaeronensis, a nephew of the famous Plutarch, and these three were the ones who wrote the present history, Sextus Chaeronensis in Greek, and the other two in Latin" (20).

Among the authentic historians named, the most important as sources are Lampridius and Julius Capitolinus, two of the *Scriptores Historiae Augustae* (abbreviated *SHA* hereafter) to whom are traditionally assigned a collection of thirty biographies of the emperors from Hadrian to Carinus. The *Vitae Caesarum,* as it was often called, was printed in 1475, 1516, and 1518, this last being the edition of Erasmus.[3] Aelius Lampridius is the supposed author of the life of Commodus, Marcus Aurelius's depraved son.

Julius Capitolinus is the author of the lives of Marcus Aurelius and his coruler Verus, among others. This life of Marcus is actually the principal source of Guevara's biographical information.

Among the "others" used by Guevara, who characterizes their works as epitomes, is Vulcacius Gallicanus, another of the *SHA,* whose life of the rebel Avidius Cassius probably suggested details to Guevara, since it contains several letters (including one from Faustina), a speech, various pronouncements, and a rather vague allusion to Marcus's book, now known as the *Meditations.*

Menéndez Pelayo believes that *The Golden Book* is, "in its general concept," an imitation of Xenophon's *Cyropedia,* which he thinks Guevara must have read in Latin translation.[4] (Guevara himself mentions the *Cyropedia* in the prologue of the *Dial of Princes.*) Marcus Aurelius's last speeches he takes to be an imitation of Cyrus's farewell to his sons, friends, and magistrates. It seems to me, however, that the king of Persia's joyous leave-taking bears only the remotest similarity to the gloomy monologue found in the final chapters of part I of the *Golden Book.* Possible points of contact are Cyrus's observations on immortality (7.19–22), on his desire to be buried directly in earth, "the mother of all beautiful things" (7.25), and the cares of kingship (7.12). Yet Guevara surely needed no model to suggest to him such topics for a dying ruler's speech. *The Golden Book* is undoubtedly, as Menéndez Pelayo says, an example of the "pedagogicopolitical" novels of which Xenophon's is the oldest in our tradition; it therefore has the family resemblance one would expect of descendants of the *Cyropedia*. But I am unconvinced that Guevara had the Greek work in mind while composing his own.[5]

The imaginary histories from which Guevara claims to have made his own compilation are attributed to three of Marcus's instructors in philosophy whose names are linked in a passage from Julius Capitolinus: "In addition, he [the emperor] attended the lectures of Sextus of Chaeronea, the nephew of Plutarch, and of Junius Rusticus, Claudius Maximus, and Cinna Catulus, all Stoics" (*SHA*, 137). It is curious to note, however, that one of Marcus's teachers, Fronto, did in fact leave a large collection of educational correspondence, most of it between himself and Marcus, and that this correspondence was not discovered until 1815.

The mention of rediscovered authentic works leads naturally to the Greek *Meditations* of Marcus himself. The collection of Stoic maxims compiled by Marcus was discovered shortly after the publication of the *Golden Book* and was edited by Xylander in 1558.

In his prologue, Guevara tells how he was led to search for the lost biography of Marcus: "While I was reading a history book one day, I found by chance a reference to this history and a letter from it quoted, and it was so good that I did everything humanly possible to find it" (21). Several of the works used by Guevara either cite or allude to lost correspondence and biography. If the fertile mind of Guevara needed anything to suggest to it the "discovery" of a forgotten account, it might have found just such a stimulus in Julius Capitolinus's life of Marcus, where the lost work of the historian Marius Maximus is cited twice, or in Vulcacius Gallicanus's life of Avidius Cassius, where Maximus's book is actually quoted several times and where four letters purported to have been written by Marcus are included as documents. Vulcacius also relates that Marcus Aurelius, before leaving for the Marcomannic war, agreed to issue his *praecepta philosophiae* and that for three days he discussed them one after the other. This rather nebulous reference to the *Meditations* might also have suggested to Guevara the "recovery" of the emperor's lost philosophical writings.

Numerous early Christian writers, who dealt kindly with the pagan Marcus, mention *litterae* (either "a letter" or "letters") dispatched to Rome by the emperor to apprise the citizens of a great victory in Hungary. During the war, the prayers of Christian soldiers had brought down a sudden thunderstorm that relieved the thirsting Roman army and frightened their barbarian attackers into flight. The *First Apology* of St. Justin Martyr (not printed, in Greek or Latin, until after Guevara's death and probably unknown to him) ends with a spurious "Letter of Marcus Aurelius to the Senate," which relates the miracle. Tertullian takes the account from Justin and alludes to "the letters of Marcus Aurelius, that most grave of emperors"; Eusebius quotes Tertullian, who said that "letters of Marcus, the most wise emperor, were even in that day still in circulation" and were proof of the miracle's authenticity. From Eusebius's *Ecclesiastical History,* this passage entered St. Prosper of Aquitain's chronology of world history and Orosius's *Seven Books against the Pagans,* both used by Guevara. So the oft-repeated words "extant litterae Marci Aurelii gravissimi imperatoris" found in standard Christian historical texts might also have put the idea into the ingenious bishop's head.

"After having looked through many books, visited many bookstores, spoken to many scholars, and searched in many kingdoms," continues Guevara, "I finally discovered it in Florence, among the books which Cosimo de' Medici (a man of respected memory, certainly) had left" (21). But the friar could scarcely have hoped to convince the circle of scholars, churchmen, and Latinists at court that he had actually discovered an authentic manuscript which (a) he had kept secret for a number of years, (b) was not willing to produce, and (c) about which the friends who helped him translate it were stubbornly silent. As indicated at the beginning of this chapter, his plain intention was to write a novelistic *regimen principum,* and the apparatus is a kind of scholarly joke which unfortunately did not amuse the learned but did sometimes deceive the unsophisticated.[6] Guevara was following the tradition of the novels of chivalry, which always

purport to be ancient books discovered under remarkable circumstances. He was merely the first well-known writer of the
Renaissance to use it for "serious" literature.

With regard to sources, then, one may say that Guevara
freely combines the bits of fact from his authentic sources (the
SHA and Herodian, principally) with fiction. For occasional
details, he goes to Orosius, *Seven Books against the Pagans* (e.g.,
for omens), or St. Augustine, *The City of God* (e.g., for the
history of the theater), or others. But in general, the plot of
the work and the characters are pure fiction.[7]

III   *Contemporary Allusions*

In the sixteenth century, the educated reader viewed history
as an inexhaustible source of cases and anecdotes which showed
him how to conduct his life. It was the historian's duty to reveal
these vital principles of history as it was the preacher's to show
the moral applicability of the most unlikely scriptures. Even
the writers of imaginary history—*historia* being the word for
both *history* and *novel* in Guevara's time—lay under the obligation to make their creations morally profitable; most of them
claim as Guevara does that their readers' souls will be im-
proved (19). It is, however, one thing to interpret real history
and quite another to invent it to suit one's purposes. Guevara
was not interested in history or archaeology for their own
sake. He had the preacher's consuming interest in *relevance,*
and one may safely assume that his satire and his precepts are
directed at contemporary moral problems. It would have been
pointless for him to invent situations which illustrated dead
issues. One may object that many of the foibles he satirizes are
traditional (e.g., avarice in old men) or so universal that it is
impossible to attribute them to special sixteenth-century circumstances. Still, there are enough demonstrable examples to make
the assumption quite plausible, I believe.

The most dramatic case is the speech of the peasant of the
Danube, which is, according to Américo Castro, a "direct allusion to what was then happening to the Indians in the Spanish
New World."[8] The bishop of Michoacan, writing to the emperor
in 1535, compares the lamentations of a Mexican Indian to the

peasant's speech, "which I once heard your majesty praise highly when I accompanied the court from Burgos to Madrid, before it was printed" (Castro, p. xv). Castro believes that the description of the beardless peasant is clearly that of an Indian and that Guevera may have written the episode as early as 1520, before the influx of gold changed the Spanish attitude toward the conquest of America.

If Castro is correct, then perhaps we may assume that the changes later made by Guevara in the description of the peasant (who in the "authorized" version has a beard and is more Germanic in appearance) respond to this revised attitude. The modifications in any case effectively conceal possible allusions to America, and the peasant's speech becomes a more general indictment of conquest, greed (the basis of conquest), and tyrannical governor-judges.

Ignorant, corrupt, and cruel judges (a term virtually interchangeable with governor, since administrative officials, together with their councillors, usually constituted a kind of court) were a constant object of Guevara's satire. In the tenth letter of *The Golden Book* he deals with the undue severity of judges in Sicily and the unrest that their strictness has caused. Marcus tells the story of a venerable Jew who spoke to the Senate, as the peasant of the Danube had done, on the cruelty of four judges, whose corruption and wicked lives had "poisoned" Palestine. As in the case of the peasant, the Senate recorded his speech and replaced the most recent of the evil judges with Pontius Pilate (a wonderful touch). Guevara's brother, a lawyer who eventually became an important member of various royal councils, had to flee Sicily in 1516 because of riots against the Spanish viceroy and high court, and it appears likely to me that Guevara is using this recent event to illustrate his theory that exemplary judges and clemency are in the long run more effective than severity, especially if the judge's habits make him unpopular.[9]

An intriguing episode, which probably refers to an as yet unidentified incident, is the expulsion of actors and entertainers. According to Guevara, Marcus Aurelius "was not fond of *pantomini* (who are the organizers of theatrical amusements) and even less of entertainers" (71). During a religious festival, two temples

vied for the services of a group of entertainers, and the uproar
which resulted caused the emperor to pack three boat loads of
actors off to a remote island. The episode is elaborated in letter
11, where Marcus accuses entertainers of "perverting judgment"
and "causing several deaths" (267). He lumps actors (*histriones*)
with the jesters and fools who surround important persons: "What
greater disgrace could there be in the capitol than the custom
of celebrating the sayings of a fool with the laughter of many
wise men? What greater scandal than that the doors of the prince's
house are always open to fools and never to sensible men? What
greater cruelty than that [princes] should give more to a fool in
one day than to their servants in a year or their relatives in all
their lives? . . . What could be more insulting to Rome than that
actors and jesters should leave greater estates and renown in
Italy with their sonnets and stories [*rodajas?*] than famous
captains? . . ." (269). The custom of keeping fools, who survive
"by sowing folly and reaping money" (269), is at least one target
of this letter. Charles V maintained, among others, a jester named
Francesillo de Zúñiga, famous for his sarcasm, who was later
murdered by an offended courtier. Guevara himself is twitted
by the jester in a burlesque chronicle which is to some extent a
parody of *The Golden Book*.[10]

Marcus's talk on the "cancer of idleness," especially when war
(e.g., the commune rebellion) disturbs the normal order, could
be copiously illustrated with passages from contemporary and
somewhat later history, biography, and fiction. The picaresque
novels, notably *Guzmán de Alfarache*, harp on the problems
created when youth are not taught useful occupations. The social
and legal disadvantages of gainful employment, the doubtful
respectability of certain professions (like medicine) and new
wealth, and many other factors favored the increase of idleness
among the upper classes and those who aspired to rise. Guevara,
through Marcus, urges the young emperor to raise the social
value of useful occupations. It is interesting that the "ancient
Roman" trades of which Marcus approved are painting, sculpting,
silversmithing, and teaching or studying; a "senator" might
pursue these employments without loss of status. He could
not be a miller, blacksmith, baker, or swineherd [*montanero?*],
because in the past members of these trades "had committed

certain treasons" (95). Guevara is suggesting that, in addition to the military skills which Spanish gentlemen were assumed to have, they should also pursue some "liberal" occupation, these being fine arts or "letters" such as legal studies. He does not take ecclesiastics into account in these remarks.

The notion that Guevara's life of Marcus began not with history but with abuses that Guevara wished to bring to the emperor's attention does not account satisfactorily for the portion of the novel that deals with education. I believe the explanation to be that Guevara hoped to present an educational program which the emperor would adopt with the future Philip II, born in 1527, one year before *The Golden Book* appeared in print. Guevara's ideas are traditional, conservative, and remain undeveloped. Perhaps he hoped to insinuate that he himself would be an excellent choice as one of the prince's tutors.

IV *Criticism*

Guevara started his career with what is, undoubtedly, his masterpiece, though the undimmed charm of lesser works like *The Art of Navigation* may appeal more to modern readers. The astounding success of *The Golden Book* cannot be attributed to any single cause, but an examination of the historical situation, of contemporary literature, and of Guevara's artistic methods suggests possible reasons.

First, the novice writer began under a remarkably favorable conjunction of circumstances. His skill as a preacher made him useful, his connections at court gave him entry to the inner circle of aristocrats and officials who surrounded Charles V, and his appointment to the royal chapel assured him a respectful public at home. The very fact that *The Golden Book* was written for the amusement of the emperor and was dedicated to him would have guaranteed the work at least an ephemeral celebrity. His association with the most cosmopolitan, influential court in Europe gave him the publicity abroad which soon made him the most widely read Spaniard of the early sixteenth century.

But it is not just the desire of provincial aristocrats and social

climbers to follow the fashions of the imperial court which was
responsible for the modest scandal that greeted the publication
of *The Golden Book*. For the work as we know it was never
published, in the modern meaning of the word, by Guevara.
It was written, like most of the "serious" prose of the world
until printing became very cheap, for a limited public who
would understand not only its conventional elements (e.g., its
learned vocabulary and syntactical peculiarities) but would
also be able to read between the lines for the doctrinal and
political intentions of the author.[11] Most of these intentions
we now overlook entirely. They were sufficiently transparent
to the readers of the sixteenth century, however, and no doubt
caused embarrassment to Guevara when three editions appeared without his authorization. Guevara later rewrote parts
of the book for its official publication, when he printed it in
1529 with the new title, the *Dial of Princes* (*Relox de príncipes*).

The most notable example of the veiled doctrinal material
which lacks its original meaning for modern readers is the
long speech made by a German peasant before the Roman
senate, a speech which so beautifully presented the ideas of
those opposed to foreign conquest that it probably circulated
apart from *The Golden Book* and, according to the prologue
of the *Dial of Princes*, was plagiarized by an as yet unidentified
author.

The incorporation of such criticisms as those cited, even when
they are couched in the most general terms, gives the book a
relevant, controversial tone which is always good publicity. This,
in the briefest possible terms, is the historical circumstance by
which Guevara profited—consciously, as an articulate moral the-
orist, writing for select ears; and unwittingly (it would seem),
as the formulator of a point of view that gained acceptance
even among audiences who probably did not understand the
direct allusions.

Another portion of *The Golden Book* that, like the peasant's
speech, also seems to have led a life of its own, is an argument
between the emperor and his wife over the key to his private
office. And it brings us to the second area in which one may
fruitfully seek the reasons for the popularity of the *Golden
Book*, namely, the purely literary area. In the prologue to the

Dial of Princes Guevara tells us that not only the *villano*'s speech but also "Marcus Aurelius's talk with Faustina, when she asked him for the key," was plagiarized and printed under another author's name.[12]

The modern reader can easily appreciate the humor of the situation without lessons in literary history. The sight of the grave philosopher-king haranguing his wife as a result of a commonplace marital disagreement is funny, slightly shocking, and surprising for the sixteenth century, though we are now familiar with the technique of bringing historical personages to life by giving them ordinary weaknesses and interesting, identifiable quirks. Guevara's method is the method of G. B. Shaw in *Caesar and Cleopatra* or Robert Graves in *I, Claudius.*

Guevara (like Shaw, especially) reduces the awesome personages of history to cranky or frivolous characters in whom we recognize humans of our own experience. The difference between Guevara's "historical" characters and those of the popular novels of chivalry is very revealing. In the latter, the pseudomedievalism, stilted language, and heroic scale of the protagonists (who are, by the conventions of the genre, all "historical") succeed only in dehumanizing them; their fantastic enemies and prodigious valor in war and love are what fascinate the reader. In *The Golden Book*, there is almost no action at all. The central characters must therefore be sufficiently interesting to attract the reader's sympathy. Guevara substituted the classical setting for the medieval, but instead of following the novel of chivalry's convention of exalting the hero or the king until he is out of touch with humanity, he lowers him until he has almost nothing of the heroic left. This technique first appears in a late medieval chivalresque novel, written in Catalan, which contains passages of unequaled brilliance that surpass every piece of Peninsular prose work except the *Celestina* until the midsixteenth century. *Tirante el blanco*, as it was known in Spanish, is too long and is extremely uneven in literary merit, but to it must be attributed the achievement of breathing life into chivalrous heroes by converting their fabulous jousts, their dreamlike love affairs, and their palling, rhetorical *courtoisie* to pointless fights, womanizing, and plain language. *Tirante* is the only contemporary work that Guevara ever mentions favorably, and he seems to have learned how to reduce his characters to human proportions from this extraordinary, neglected book. But Guevara, like many readers of his day, probably found *Tirante* wanting on moral grounds, for it is certainly the most obscene book in Spanish (though others claim this dubious honor). At the relatively strait-laced court of Charles V, Amadís de Gaula, with his manly sentimentality, became the gentleman's model. Tirante is not elegant enough. Yet for all its popularity, *Amadís* has no better character portrayals than *The Golden Book.* Amadís and Oriana are too predictable, even though on occasion, amid the declamations of noble sentiments and grand passions, they spring to life for a moment The *Amadís* has aged better than *The Golden Book* for other reasons, principally because its fantasy is eternal, while the faddish classicism of Guevara's work has become merely quaint.

Along with *The Golden Book* and *Amadís*, the third literary success of the early sixteenth century, and the greatest of all, is the *Celestina.* But the *Celestina* comes of a different line; it is a prose drama about a bourgeois tragedy. Plain language and vulgar affairs came naturally to the *Celestina* from the Latin comedies. Guevara, in contrast, was dealing with kings and aristocrats and is therefore closer to the tradition of the novel of chivalry and to *Amadís.* His diffuse style is the very opposite of the concentrated brilliance of Rojas's deft portraits.

In sum, it is Guevara's skillful combination of aristocratic subject matter—which is at the same time "historical" and edifying—with the techniques of realism usually applied to non-aristocratic subject matter (learned possibly from *Tirante,* perhaps from the *Celestina,* perhaps from that master of the chatty monologue, the Archpriest of Talavera) which attracted the sixteenth-century reader.

Having looked at the possible antecedents of the techniques of character-creation which fray Antonio uses in his novel, let us look at the characters themselves and at what Guevara does and does not do with his historical material.

Any educated person, even if he is not particularly well-versed in classical matters, has some notion of, for example, the character of the emperor Nero. One's ability to visualize Nero at all has been greatly developed by the cinema, and he probably has a rather correct impression of the "archaeological" aspects of Nero's epoch. The genteel readers of the Renaissance were exposed to a great deal more classical history and literature, but it is questionable whether they had a better grasp of it, since they tended to see antiquity in terms of their own civilization, with little concept of the deep cultural gulf between themselves and the ancient Romans. A good example of this anachronism is the frontispiece of the 1529 Zaragoza edition of *The Golden Book* (reproduced by Castro), which shows a crowned ruler, identified as "Marcus Aurelius the Emperor" holding orb and scepter, surrounded by noblemen in Renaissance costume.

The educated man of Guevara's time also had stereotyped notions of great historical figures, and to him Marcus Aurelius was the philosopher-emperor, known for his gentleness and (on the testimony of the church fathers) his tolerance of Christians. Guevara, therefore, would have to work with the popular concept of Marcus Aurelius in mind, as scenario writers use the popular concept of Nero, balancing familiar traits with enough new material to keep the reader interested. Guevara's main source of information, the Roman historian Julius Capitolinus, presents Marcus as a kindly intellectual, "devoted to philosophy as long as he lived and preeminent among emperors for purity of life." This ardor for philosophy "made him serious and dignified, not ruining, however, a certain geniality in him, which he manifested toward his household, his friends, and even to those less intimate, making him, rather, austere, though not unreasonable, modest, though not inactive, and serious without gloom" (*SHA*, 143). When at eighteen he was made an adopted grandson by the emperor Hadrian, he accepted this elevation reluctantly, enumerating "the evil things that sovereignty involved" (*ibid*). He so won the respect and affection of Antoninus Pius that Pius confirmed him as successor. Marcus, however, immediately made his adopted brother Lucius coruler. As the more influential of the two rulers, Marcus set the tone of the empire: "He was at all times exceedingly reasonable both in restraining men from evil and in urging them to good, generous in rewarding and quick to forgive, thus making bad men good, and good men very good, and he even bore with unruffled temper the insolence of not a few" (*SHA*, 163). But, as Capitolinus

says, "there is no emperor who is not the victim of some evil
tale, and Marcus is no exception" (*SHA*, 171). He was accused
not only of poisoning his stepbrother but also of selfish indifference to his wife's supposed adulteries, since it was through
her (as daughter of Antoninus Pius) that he had come to the
throne. Faustina is even said to have encouraged a rebellion,
led by Avidius Cassius, against Marcus.

In the original sources Marcus, except where juicy gossip is
reported about him, is rather colorless. It is interesting to
observe how Guevara alters the historical Marcus. He sets the
stage by simplifying the scenery: first, Marcus's coemperor Verus
disappears. Guevara may have eliminated him for purely artistic reasons, such as a desire to limit the principals to two. But
there is also the interesting possibility that Verus was sacrificed
for more delicate reasons: Charles V as the recipient of the
work must have been constantly before the friar's eyes as he
worked. Charles's younger brother Fernando had been reared
in Spain, spoke Spanish, and was popular among the people.
In fact, the move to set him on the Spanish throne and leave
Charles the foreign domains was so strong that Charles's advisers got him out of the country in order to prevent a con-
frontation (cf. Sandoval I, 118 ff., 134 ff.). It would have been
impolitic for Guevara to propose as a pattern for Charles's
actions a ruler who voluntarily divided his empire with his
adopted brother, and I am inclined to feel that this explains the
suppression of Verus.

The rebellion of Avidius Cassius is also suppressed. Again, the
reasons are perhaps only artistic; but there is also the possibility
that, so soon after the *comunero* rebellions, Guevara preferred not
to have his hero—whose actions he commends to Charles as
worthy of imitation—either forgive ex-rebels (thereby confirming
their guilt and exalting Marcus's clemency) or dispense stern
justice. There were interested parties at court who might well
be offended at either solution. Faustina's immorality is of course
eliminated, though Guevara gives her sufficient willfulness to
allow Marcus scope for his theories on the ways of women. As
a substitute, the bishop exaggerated or invented conflicts between
Faustina and Marcus over the education and marriage of the
children. Guevara also maintains carefully the pagan tone of the

work and never alludes to the famous miracle which is reported at length in Dio and is mentioned by so many Christian writers.

Once he has reduced the background to its barest essentials, he presents Marcus in a series of disconnected episodes. These "scenes" allow the emperor to reveal himself, through his speeches and, later, his letters. The expressionless, stoical Marcus of history discloses unsuspected facets of his personality in youthful *billets-doux*. This psychological richness in the imaginary Marcus not only shows great skill in the creation of fictional characters, but it is particularly original as a recreation of a historical personality.

In book one, along with the new-found sharpness of the emperor's tongue, his characteristic style (which later turns out to be Guevara's style, though, except for those who had heard his sermons, this fact was unknown), and the concrete, picturesque details of his life and relationships—all of which go far to quicken the imaginary emperor—the most important addition is what might be called the incompatibility of Marcus and Faustina. The classical historians were not kind to Faustina. The exaggerated contrasts between her libidinous activities and conspiracy with Avidius Cassius (reported as unverified rumors) and the purity and guilelessness of Marcus suggest that the differences are more dramatic than real. Guevara, who loved dramatic contrasts to such an extent that there is scarcely a sentence in his writings that does not include one, could hardly resist such an opportunity to play the severe emperor against the frivolous empress. He rejects the sinful actions hinted at, or reported by, the historians but retains Faustina's dubious reputation. Julius Capitolinus hardly mentions Faustina except in connection with her reported adulteries and the rebellion. He records, however, that when Marcus married his daughter Lucilla to Claudius Pompeianus, a man "advanced in years, a native of Antioch, whose birth was not sufficiently noble" (*SHA*, 183), Faustina and Lucilla were both opposed to this match. Vulcacius Gallicanus cites letters to prove that Faustina was not only *not* in collusion with Cassius, but that she was a faithful, solicitous wife, concerned for her children's future (*SHA*, 183). In one letter cited by him, Faustina speaks of family illnesses and problems with doctors; she has not been able to meet Marcus "because our dear Fadilla was ill" (255). She wants another physician because her own "does not know how to treat a young girl." From these passages, Guevara takes the idea that Faustina was inclined to spoil her children and that she worked without Marcus Aurelius's knowledge to promote splendid marriages for her daughters. The education of the children forms the base of the imaginary contest between Marcus and Faustina.

Guevara makes poor Faustina an emotional, stubborn woman whose well-meaning but unwise actions bring down her husband's withering scorn but never a glimmer of sympathy. She is a nebulous, rather pitiful figure. And her fate seems all the sadder in that her death is not even recorded. Marcus mentions, quite casually, his second wife in one place and commends her to his friends on his deathbed. The historical Marcus did not remarry.[13]

Guevara's indifference to strict chronology and his preference for an episodic rather than a linear biographical approach is one important indication of his artistic—as opposed to a historical —approach to the character. The use of speeches, questions which elicit long, speechlike replies—in short, the absence of real dialogue—combine with the virtual absence of action to make a static, slowly developing piece of work that often tires with its repetitions and heavy-handed use of showy rhetoric. Guevara, however, had the interesting and original idea of placing the "rediscovered" correspondence of Marcus in a separate collection, as book II of his novel. There are numerous popular antecedents which might also have suggested to Guevara the use of the epistolary form for novelistic purposes.[14]

The reader finds that these letters approach in many cases the same subject matter found in part one. But as letters they are a much more realistic, plausible, acceptable form of oratory and do not have the same hieratic effect that an identical speech does when "spontaneously" made by Marcus in reply to a question. Indeed, the apparently natural effect of a collection of carefully written letters on different subjects gives the reader a second wind. And it has two curious effects which have as yet not been diminished by imitation. First, the letters create in the reader a strong feeling that he himself is recalling their antecedents and background. This is done by carefully chosen, seemingly offhand allusions to circumstances which are only partly revealed in the letter itself. Secondly, the letters intensify the realism of the characters (mainly that of Marcus) in a natural fashion, by presenting an anecdote a second time from a different point of view. The "perspectivism" is a foreshadowing of the possibilities realized by Cervantes some seventy years later.[15]

The only really new subject matter introduced in the letters is Marcus's youthful love life. The love letters and spiteful exchanges add a last, unsuspected facet to the personality of the emperor and provide a kind of surprise ending.

Letter 13 is Marcus's reply to seven Roman ladies of dubious virtue who, at the Roman equivalent of Mardi Gras, have satirized him and displayed a scarecrowlike effigy of him with a placard that said "His life is fuller of hypocrisies than this statue is of different materials" (281). Marcus's reply begins in a good-natured tone but ends with an insult for each of the wretched ladies: Abilina sells virgins; Toringa needs a *modius* of peas to count her numerous lovers; Rotoria spent two years on a pirate ship with an exclusive franchise to service one hundred sailors, etc., etc. The reader of all this is not only surprised at the sudden turn the letter takes but is curious to know why a group of courtesans would satirize a scholarly philosopher away studying rhetoric in Rhodes; why they find a discrepancy between his opinion of women and his behavior; and how he is so familiar with the antics of lovers and with the intimate secrets of a sizable group of whores. Subsequent letters provide answers to some of these questions.

The next two, numbers 14 and 15, are an exchange between Marcus, the heir apparent, and his former mistress Bohemia. In spite of the balanced sentences of Marcus's letter, it conveys a tone of authentic regret and bitterness, of sour pleasure in insulting the aging courtesan. Guevara illustrates in a very lively if disagreeable way how one's chickens always come home to roost. Both Marcus and Bohemia are paying for the sexual excesses of their younger days, Marcus with anguish and guilt, Bohemia with shame, poverty, and ill health. Marcus, however, has extracted himself from the slavery of the senses by an act of will and keeps himself free by the exercise of reason. He provides an edifying example of the moral uprightness, not super-

human purity, accessible to all reasonable men. Bohemia in
contrast is a sad case of the sensual woman who is constantly
buffeted by desire and resentment.

Bohemia's reply is a masterpiece of poisonous sarcasm, a line-
by-line commentary on Marcus's letter. Her version of Marcus's
love affair with her and other women reminds the reader of the
unspecified accusations of the seven ladies of letter 13. The letter
is the best example of Guevara's technique of presenting two
sides of a story and leaving the reader to draw his own conclusions. There is never any doubt that Marcus, at least as emperor,
is a man of great moral stature. But as a lover, Bohemia's pas-
sionate vilification raises some doubt in the reader's mind.

According to the letter, Marcus offered himself to Bohemia's
father as a reading teacher, seduced her, promised to marry her,
and then jilted her. Nor was she the only victim of his innocent
appearance: "The matrons of Rome had discovered a fine watch-
dog for their daughters in you!" (297). But, says Bohemia in an
exultant tone, "I have only to see you married to Faustina, and
I am revenged..." (298). She closes with the supreme sarcasm
of which the Romance vocabulary of obscene innuendo is capable: "We are obliged to you for one thing, namely the example
of long-suffering which you set for us all, for since you tolerate
such notorious infamy in Faustina, it is little enough for us to
tolerate a few secret sins in you..." (301).

As Marcus's and Bohemia's letters referred to Marcus's youth,
so the next pair, 16 and 17, continue the flashback. They are relics
of an affair, or of an attempt by Marcus to start an affair, with a
married woman named Macrina, full of the phrases of courtly
love. The reader learns that Marcus, a judge, saw Macrina on
his way to a public hanging and immediately fell in love with
her: "... what kind of justice is this, that kills men who steal
money and tolerates ladies who steal hearts?" (302). Macrina
does not read his letters, listen to his go-betweens, or acknowledge his love tokens. The affair with Macrina apparently stopped
at this point, for Marcus was on the verge of a far more serious
moral infraction than concubinage, which after all was accepted
by the pagan world, as Guevara's readers knew.

The young philosopher Marcus accidentally drops a letter in
the temple of the Vestal Virgins and returns to look for it. He

sees Libia standing before the goddess pouring out offerings of oil and honey and immediately loves her. "I am amazed at myself," says Marcus in a letter to her (no. 18), "because I thought that temptations did not come to men in the temple of the Vestal Virgins" (307). And, he adds, "I suppose, Lady Libia, that you will be amazed, because while everyone sees me outwardly a philosopher, you know me to be secretly in love. I beg you not to give me away, because if the gods grant me a long life, I hope to mend my ways, and though I am a foolish youth, I shall be a wise old man" (308).

Marcus avers that however wise, however indifferent to the world a philosopher may be, he can never control his instincts completely, though he may suppress his desire with virtuous intentions; indeed, "the man who is not a lover can only be a fool" (309). He begs Libia to accept his love and to tell him frankly how she feels. He sends her a golden ribbon as a token.

Perhaps the reader, knowing this to be a fiction by a friar, would find the expression of Platonic love piquant, though such expressions from churchmen (e.g., Bembo or Pius II) were hardly a novelty to Guevara's audience. The line "under their rough vesture, their flesh is very soft" (308–9) might apply to a Franciscan, accustomed to wearing a cheap, coarse habit. But it seems to me to be rather a predictable contrast typical of Guevara's illustrations: no matter how spiritual a man, he must make continual war on his instincts. Any refined reader of the sixteenth century would be bound to agree that the man incapable of love is a fool. But susceptibility to love, which is a good thing, does not mean surrender to love, which may be bad. The shy, gentle tenor of this letter contrasts with the brash aggressiveness of the letters to Macrina and sounds even more youthful.

Guevara suppressed these letters in the *Dial of Princes*, and in his *Familiar Letters* (I, 64) deplores having published such "vanities." His artist's pride in the success of the letters is compatible with repentance for possible sins they may have inspired "and the bad example which I set." But he does not drop the pose of translator even in his epistles, where he says that he still has "a reasonable quantity" of Marcus's love letters, but only a few of those "which are moral and of sound doctrine" (Cossío ed., I, 451, 452).

Whatever the possible embarrassment the letters may have caused a rising churchman, they are logically and aesthetically sound as part of *The Golden Book*. (Publishers and public continued to like them, and they were usually appended to the *Dial of Princes*, from which, of course, they had been expurgated.) In context they seem to be all the more effective, because their moral lesson is implicit. First, all of the love letters present the traditional foibles of youth and early manhood which the emperor has overcome by sheer reason and will; he is, after all, a pagan without the revealed morality of Christianity. There is also the possibility that Guevara placed them, especially the florid, cliché-ridden letters to Macrina, at the end of the novel as ironic proof of the inherent silliness of courtly love conventions. The dying, weeping lover, who penned the ritual declamations of eternal fidelity, imminent death, suffering, etc. ("I shall never lose hope"; "it is just for me to die for you"; "you have destroyed my person") was still alive and well forty years later, and the affair would have been forgotten—as it is omitted in the first part of the novel—but for the accident which preserved an old letter.

The exaggerated passions of courtly love were the ordinary subject of sentimental fiction in Guevara's day, and every writer of love stories insists on the exemplary nature of his works; the courtly lover (Marcus) inevitably pays for his lust (as in the case of Macrina), even if he never commits a sin of the flesh (as he does with Bohemia). Whether modern readers are convinced by such protestations of the social utility of literature, there is abundant evidence that the *possible* exemplariness of even the most scabrous love stories was seriously pondered by sixteenth-century readers. One may also consider the love material as a suggestive but undeveloped explanation of Marcus's personal problems in later life. The virtuous ruler's existence is blighted by a frivolous—possibly immoral—wife, the death of his good son, and a monster for an heir. For the moralist, Marcus is paying for the sins of his youth. If his wife is a suspected adulteress, it is because Marcus himself once pursued the "inexorable" wife of another man.

CHAPTER 3

The Dial of Princes

I Contents

THE printer Nicolas Tierri, in early April, 1529, issued from his press in Valladolid a fat volume of over three hundred folios with the following title: *A Book Called A CLOCK FOR PRINCES, which incorporates the very famous book MARCUS AURELIUS: the author of both books is the very reverend father Friar Antonio de Guevara, preacher and chronicler of his majesty, now bishop-elect of Guadix: the author warns the reader to read the prologues first, if he wishes to understand the books.*[1]

The docile reader who heeds Guevara's warning soon finds himself wandering in a maze of loosely connected thoughts on man's eternal dissatisfaction. Most believe, says the bishop-elect (with irritating amplitude) that only the prince is fortunate. The truth of the matter is, however, that the privileges of rulership are overshadowed by the cares of government; indeed, if rulers knew how sweet it is to live in peace, they would envy the lowly. But the prince must accept his responsibilities and must set an example, "for the entire republic is measured by the life of the prince" (2r).

Guevara is cognizant of the dangers of writing a book for princes and great lords, but he states cautiously that he is not going to offend them with criticism but to exhort them to virtue. With good humor, he compares himself to the philosopher Phorvión (i.e., Phormio) who displayed his book-learned knowledge of warfare before Hannibal. When Phorvión's proud patron asked Hannibal what he thought of the speech, Hannibal asked how "a wretched little man like this, reared all his life in a corner of Greece studying philosophy" dared even to discuss war before a real general (2v). Your Majesty may well ask,

53

says Guevara to the emperor, who gave me the courage to write about something of which I have no experience; in fact, the less I know of the world, the better I am as a monk. But as a humble servant of your Majesty I am obliged to offer my advice. Furthermore, there is the precedent set by Xenophon and Onesicritus who both wrote books of instruction for rulers, though they were not princes themselves; and they each use the literary device of a prince teaching his son, "because it seemed to those philosophers that that writing had no authority if it did not go in the name of those princes who had experience of that of which they were writing" (3v).

Guevara ends the "General Prologue" with an explanation of the unusual title of the book. Just as clocks were introduced in antiquity in order to regulate the activities of the republic, so his book is a "clock of life," a *Clock for Princes*, which tells not time but "how we are to occupy ourselves every hour and how we are to order our lives" (7v).

Next come the preface and argument from *The Golden Book*, with interesting changes and additions, including the story of how the original came to be printed.

I began to devote my attention to this book in 1518; and no one knew what I was working on until 1524 [1523?]: the next year, 1524, since the book which I had kept so secret was made known, his majesty, who was ill with quartern fever, asked me for it in order to pass the time and alleviate his fever.[2] I presented his majesty with *Marcus Aurelius*, which I had neither finished nor corrected, and I asked him humbly for no other favor in recompense for my labor than that he not allow anyone in his chamber an opportunity to copy it, because, since I was still working on it, it was not my intention to publish it as it then was; otherwise, his majesty would be ill served and I would be harmed. But for my sins, the book was stolen and by divers persons handed about and copied; some stole it from others, and it was copied by pageboys. Since the number of mistakes in it increased daily and there was only one original by which to correct them, a number of persons actually brought me some of the copies to correct. If the copies could have talked, they would have complained more of those who wrote them than I did of those who had stolen it! While one error was being added to another and I was finishing my book and ready to publish it, *Marcus Aurelius* suddenly appeared in print in Seville. . . . Another thing happened with *Marcus*

Aurelius which it pains me to mention—and which those who did it should be ashamed of having done—namely, that various people passed themselves off as the authors of the whole work; others inserted parts of it into their own works as if it were theirs, as appears in one printed book where the author put the peasant's speech; and another author in another book, also printed, put the speech which Marcus Aurelius made to Faustina when she asked him for the key. (13v–14r)[3]

The correctness, completeness, and increase in size of the *Dial of Princes* all prove that "my principal intention was not to translate *Marcus Aurelius*[4] but to make *A Clock for Princes* by which all christendom may be guided.... This *Clock for Princes* is divided into three books: the first tells how the prince should be a good Christian; the second, how the prince should behave with his wife and children; and the third, how he should govern his person and his republic. I had begun another book on how the prince should deal with his court and household, but the excessive insistence of friends that I publish this book made me arrest my pen" (14r).

The first three chapters of the *Dial* present, in expanded and rearranged form, the lineage and youth of Marcus found in chapters 1–2 of *The Golden Book*. Anecdotes, laws, and letters brief and lengthy are sprinkled liberally over the plainer prose of the first version. The longest addition concerns a provincial innkeeper who tells a visiting censor how Rome's policies and the civil wars of Marius and Sulla have devastated the country and corrupted the customs of the people. The story illustrates Marcus's observations on the decline of virtue as a result of lax parental discipline and of innovations; this is the first example of many in which a simple man, like the peasant of the Danube, rebukes the decadent ways of "Rome."

Chapters 4 through 16 explore aspects of the subject of book I of *The Dial of Princes,* that the prince must be a Christian. Guevara discusses the vanity of the innumerable gods of paganism, the majesty and miracles of the one true God, the excellence of Christianity, and God's favor to truly Christian rulers like the emperor Valens.

Chapters 17-27 treat of the duty of the prince to protect and encourage religion; there are examples of the disastrous effects of impiety and heresy as well as of the rewards of piety. The chapters begin with a new letter in which Marcus Aurelius gives his opinions of religion ("the virtues of the man who is neglectful of his gods are to be considered vices"). Guevara explains that God rewarded the good intentions of pagan Romans with material prosperity; he warns his princely readers by means of examples from pagan history, the Old Testament, and early Christian history that "God punishes those who do not respect his temples"; and as a final illustration of the ideal interaction of the secular and ecclesiastical duties of the prince, he excerpts the decrees of the hitherto unknown "Council of Hippo," presided over by a Christian king of Africa, Hismaro, and Bishop Silvanus of Carthage.

Chapters 28–34 take up the origins of monarchy, servitude, and tyranny. Man's sinful, envious nature produced the conditions under which tyranny originated (with Nimrod, according to the true account, states Guevara). Monarchy, in which "one cares for all and all obey one," is the best protection against tyranny. Alexander, with his senseless conquests, typifies the classical tyrant, and his crimes against humanity are laid before him by another "villano del Danubio." Alexander learns that the protection of national traditions, the encouragement of piety, and the suppression of envy and greed are the best ways to maintain the state.

Chapters 35–40 define the duties of the prince, which are essentially to protect true religion, help the helpless, reward the good, and punish the wicked. Guevara, using the ancient metaphor of the *corpus mysticum* of the state, discusses the importance of obedience on the part of the subject, communicability on the part of the prince. Marcus Aurelius illustrates the moral and practical rewards of kindliness, affability, and gratitude to faithful friends and servants. Chapters 41–42 discuss the disadvantages of handsomeness—which "is the mother of many vices and the stepmother of all virtues"—in princes. Guevara brings forth a new letter of Marcus Aurelius's to a playboy nephew, in which the philosopher reminds the youth that bodily charms fade with alarming speed. Chapters 43–47 take up the need of the prince to surround himself with learned men; the prince should seek out these sages, because he and his household must set an example for the entire kingdom.

Book II has as its title "The Way Princes and Great Lords Should Behave Toward Their Wives and How They Should Raise Their Children." The first three chapters cover the political and emotional benefits of marriage in princes and the history of the institution. The next chapters (4–8) are addressed to highborn ladies. The advice which they contain can be distilled into two basic precepts: (1) love and obey your husband and (2) mind your own business. Guevara shows sympathy for the woman married to a difficult husband, but he frankly considers such a husband the woman's cross to bear. The best way for a woman to avoid temptations and discontent is for her to have as little contact with the world outside her house as possible.

Successful pregnancy is the topic of chapters 9–12 (avoid violent exercise, overeating, tight clothing, emotional shocks, etc.). These chapters lead naturally to an illustration of how the ideal prince handles the whims of a pregnant wife, to wit, the famous argument between Marcus Aurelius and Faustina over the key to the study (13–17). Guevara favors breast-feeding by the mother (18–19) but gives advice on the selection of wet nurses in cases of need (20) as well as on weaning and superstitious cures for childhood ailments (22–24).

Early in life, the (male) child should learn to speak well; even his nurses must be intelligent enough to teach him good speech (25–26). Princesses and great ladies ought also to teach their daughters: "if boys and girls studied in the same way, there would be as many wise women as there are foolish men" (116v). In antiquity, women were marvelously erudite: Sulla's daughter was a teacher of Latin and Greek, Pythagoras's sister was an authoress, the mother of the Gracchi taught philosophy at Rome. A letter from this famous lady embodies all the eloquence and sound notions of child-rearing desirable in the ideal mother (chapters 27–31).

Beginning with chapter 32, fray Antonio expounds his theory of pedagogy, namely, that example and stern discipline are the best ways to produce the self-control and temperance which are especially desirable in rulers (32–39). A good tutor should be—among other things—a man of experience (between forty and sixty), upright, eloquent, and well-read so that he can illustrate his lessons with historical examples (34). Unfortunately, the important post of royal tutor often goes to unworthy persons as a reward for services or even for payment. Marcus Aurelius had, of course, to deal with an extreme case in his own son Commodus, whose evil inclinations appeared early. (The selection and dismissal of Commodus's tutors are in chapters 35-36.) In a new speech, entitled "Ad sapientes pedagogos," Marcus analyzes the defects of "Roman" education: most young men go to school to learn to speak well in public; when they finish their studies, if they can argue and speak Latin and Greek well, their parents consider their money well spent, even if the boy is foolish and vice-ridden. Marcus wants his son to surpass others in quiet behavior, good works, and patience. Guevara concludes book II (chapters 39–40) with a note on four vices—lying, a taste for gambling, impudence, and sensuality—which aristocrats must take extra care to eradicate in their children: "... today many fathers are proud that their sons are successful with women" and delight in their bastard grandchildren; mothers "cover up the peccadillos of their sons, find nurses for the children of their son's mistresses, pay their debts when they are in debt, give them money to gamble at the gaming-tables, reconcile them with their fathers when they are angry with them, borrow money to bail them out when they are arrested, [and yet] are always annoyed with their neighbors because they do not restrain *their* sons ..." (201v).

Book III deals with "the particular virtues that princes must have," beginning with justice (chapters 1–11). The prince must "give to each what belongs to him by right and dispossess those who possess something unjustly" (203v). He must defend the common good; protect the innocent, ignorant, poor, and orphaned; restrain the greedy and ambitious; and honor the virtuous. The pursuit of justice should produce morality and peace; the punishment of criminals is to be left to executioners. Judges, the prince's delegates, must be persons of integrity, disinterested, merciful, diligent. The speeches of the German peasant and the Jew show the harm which bad judges can work (chapters 3–5, 10).

The second virtue in a prince is love of peace (12–16). It is of course his duty to defend his people. But Christians are not free to shed even the blood of enemies "for any temporal cause" (228v). Marcus's letter to his friend Cornelius appears here, with additions. In it, Marcus reveals his feelings about a victory parade, contrasting the pomp of the celebration with the hardships of war, the miseries of the vanquished, the moral damage done to the victors, the instability of fortune, etc.

Beginning with chapter 17, Guevara starts a detour which will lead (as the reader eventually finds) to the prince's third virtue, generosity. The logic seems to be that as youth is ignorant and sensual, so old age has its special vices, notably avarice; and avarice is a defect intolerable in princes, who must embody generosity and magnanimity. Guevara's beating about the bush allows him to include reflections on contemporary decadence, when venerable gentlemen dress like foppish boys, and on aristocrats who become merchants or moneylenders and abandon their hereditary duties as defenders of the state. These ideas, as well as his views on generosity in the ruler, find support in various letters written by Marcus Aurelius and in a number of classical anecdotes (chapters 17–31). Compassion for the defenseless, especially widows, is another important virtue—a virtue displayed by the philosophical Roman emperor in a letter to a noble widow (35–38). Equally important in a prince is detachment from worldly possessions controlled by Fortune (39–41).

The last virtue, though Guevara actually does not give it a name, is gravity, or perhaps sobriety, in relation to amusements and especially to the professional wits and entertainers whose presence in great households was a sign of status (42–47).

The last portion of the book recounts the exemplary death of the Roman emperor, prefaced by a short "art of dying" for princes. This time, unlike the procedure of *The Golden Book*, there are no frivolous *billets-doux* to counterbalance the solemnity of the death scene.

II *Sources*

A list of the sources and possible sources of the new material in *The Dial of Princes*—that is, material not found in *The Golden Book*—makes very dull reading even when pared to the bone.

Menéndez Pelayo noted many years ago that Plutarch's moral treatises (as well as his biographies) had obviously contributed anecdotes, as had Diogenes Laertius's *Lives of the Philosophers* and the apochryphal letters of famous Greeks like the tyrant Phalaris, one of Guevara's favorite characters. Guevara also made use of information found in Pliny's *Natural History*, Valerius Maximus's collection of witty sayings, a number of Latin historians (e.g., Caesar), essayists (e.g., Aulus Gellius), poets, Christian writers like Paulus Diaconus, Lactantius, and Isidore, and a few moderns like Giovanni Nanni, who, like Guevara, had "discovered" the lost historical works of Berosus the Chaldean and dedicated his edition to the Catholic Monarchs. Readers interested in the identification of sources should consult the Latin translation of Johann Wanckel.[5] Wanckel was a fabulously erudite man who missed very few of the classical and early Christian sources, so far as I have been able to ascertain, and who provided parallel passages in ancient and modern literatures. The edition is itself a triumph of seventeenth-century printing (in various sizes of Roman and italic types, Fraktur, and Greek).

III   *Changes and Additions*

The most obvious difference between *The Golden Book* and *The Dial of Princes* is, of course, the length of the new work, which is at least three times that of the original. The additions follow logically from the new focus of the book, which is no longer a "translation" of a pagan biography but a *doctrinal de príncipes* written for rulers, the upper nobility, and indeed for all Christendom (*todo el pueblo cristiano*). However, Guevara does not entirely abandon his pose as translator: "I put one or two chapters of my own, and then I put some letters by Marcus Aurelius or the teachings of some other ancient author.... for though the style of the Spanish is mine, I admit that most of what is said is someone else's" (14r).

The method, which fray Antonio describes accurately, is to take certain successful passages from *The Golden Book* and expand them in two ways, first by amplifying the passages themselves, multiplying examples, etc., and second, by using them as the central episodes of one of the larger clusters of chapters, providing them with what amount to prologues. For instance, the speech to Faustina becomes the final illustration of the section which deals with the relationship between the prince and his wife; the *villano's* speech becomes the climax of the chapters on justice and governors.

He perfects other techniques which appear somewhat hesitantly in *The Golden Book*. Marcus Aurelius, the solemn philosopher-emperor, appears in the original version in the unexpected role of lover and satirist. Guevara expunges the offensive love element and softens the rivalry between Marcus and Faustina over the upbringing of their children. But he uses the trick of providing some startling new information (without a basis in history) about the minor characters of the *Dial*. The proverbially cruel Phalaris, who cooked Daedalus in the bronze bull which the great craftsman had made for him, becomes "unique in his love and friendship for philosophers and learned men" (12r). Croesus and Alexander are uncharacteristically docile before the aggressive personal criticism of poor philosophers and barbarians. Guevara often pairs off historical figures as representations of opposing tendencies: Alexander versus Darius (power versus wisdom) or Midas versus Sileno, a fictitious philosopher (riches versus detachment).

One may deduce from the greatly expanded version of the ceremonial apology for errors (cf. *Golden Book*, 14–15) that Guevara's fictitious history and his style had not met with unqualified praise. The tone of the new apology is much more defensive: "I willingly confess that I do not deserve to be counted among the great sages for what I have written or translated or compiled; because (excluding holy scripture) there is nothing in the world so carefully written that it does not need revision and polishing. . . .If anyone be found who is very skilled in the Latin language, very polished in Spanish, well-grounded in history, quite expert in Greek, and very careful in searching out and examining books, not only will I permit this heroic person to correct my work, but I shall beg him to tread my teachings under his feet, because it is no affront to the humble and virtuous to be corrected by a wise man" (13r).

Another important element in his apology is fray Antonio's

claim that *The Golden Book* was incomplete and that he had
not authorized publication. This naturally relieves him of
responsibility for misinterpretation and errors. We may grant
that Guevara did not publish the book, as he says. But to all
appearances, it is complete, and it has an artistic unity which
the *Dial* lacks in large part. Furthermore, the original prologue
of *The Golden Book* is addressed not only to Charles but also
to an audience of learned readers; it is difficult to see how
it can be a premature version of a prologue for the as yet
unfinished *Dial*. There are no purely literary reasons for
Guevara to have made any changes, since *The Golden Book*
was an immediate success. He might have wanted to publish
an edition with his name as author (the three spurious editions
are anonymous), and it is conceivable that he thought such
a work would be more attractive if he could claim that it was
better and more complete than the others.

But the simplest explanation for the changes and additions
would seem to be that the pagan tone of the book and the
indecorous love letters—however harmless both elements may
seem to modern readers—provoked the disapproval of men
whose esteem Guevara courted. A monk from a conservative
order that considered the preaching of repentance its special
mission might well be embarrassed by the writing of un-
Christian fiction (which moralists considered to be a pernicious
form of lying, hardly justified even by the ethical benefits it
might confer). A man who preached to the courtiers during
Lent and on feast days might find his moral authority diminished by a collection of elegant love letters, even if they were
imaginary. And the humanists, whose territory Guevara had
invaded, had nothing but contempt for his efforts.

Guevara could satisfy critics and salvage his pride if he
claimed that it was all a misunderstanding: the pagan philosophy was merely part of a larger work of sound Christian
doctrine; the naughty letters were, after all, not the work of
Guevara; he had only translated them. And the moral intention
of the complete work should override any objections to the
fictions and inventions that he might employ as ornaments.
Besides the additions, seen above in the summary of the *Dial*,
there are many minor changes in the text as well. Most of

them seem to be insignificant, but a few are interesting. A reference to the American gold (the virtuous reader will prize *The Golden Book* as princes value the discovery of gold mines in the Indies) is omitted, perhaps because it made a tactless comparison between virtuous readers and greedy princes. The description of the *villano del Danubio* is modified to make him more Germanic; the original description did not mention a beard. The anecdote of the Jew who came to Rome to complain of the cruelty of a judge has changes that have led one scholar to see allusions to the Spanish Inquisition.[6] In the long talk between Marcus and his wife over the key to the study (an argument which takes place in private, be it remembered), there is an addition which suggests that the original version of the speech had stirred up some resentment in the hearts of female readers: "I am aware, Faustina, that you and others like you will hate me for what I have said and for what I intend to say ... but I swear by the immortal gods that in this case my object is none other than to advise good women—for there are many good women—and castigate bad women—for there are many bad women. And if by chance neither the good nor the bad are willing to believe that I have good intentions when I say what I do, I shall not for that reason cease to recognize the good among the bad..." (104r). Book III, chapter 25, is a letter in which the emperor excoriates a friend who has gone into business, thereby losing his honor and blackening the family escutcheon. In the *Dial,* the contempt for merchants is softened: "I mean, it was infamous for you, who were a warrior: for it is honorable in the republic for those who are born to the office. It is not my object, Cincinnatus, to condemn trade or merchants or to speak ill of those who buy or those who sell ... [for] it is not possible to live in the republic without merchants" (252v).

And there are a few small additions to the biography of Marcus Aurelius. Chapters 17 and 18 of Book I of the *Dial* allude to a number of episodes in the life of the young Marcus, as a scholar, soldier, and, for nine months, a galley slave of pirates. Chapter 42 adds details of his family and his adoption of a worthless but good-looking nephew, whose education he paid for by teaching. In Book II, chapter 13, we learn that

Marcus's son-in-law Pompeianus deposited the writings of the
dead emperor in the Capitol, "where the Romans honored
them as Christians honor holy relics" (292r), and that these
writings all perished when the Goths destroyed Rome.

The most puzzling additions are the fake "authorities," or
what in a modern book of semischolarly pretensions would be
hundreds of footnotes citing nonexistent works. In *The Golden
Book*, the use of fictitious anecdotes or sayings attributed to
imaginary writers or works is a consequence of the basic fiction
and has antecedents in other works which purport to be historical. If in the *Dial* Guevara had merely incorporated his original
fiction, which was already a literary success, or had confined
new falsifications to longer anecdotes, his "honesty" would
never have been called into question. But the staggering pro-
fusion of fake attributions is unnecessary. Indeed, one feels
that it is even inconsistent with the intentions of the revised
work, and it seems out of character for a serious churchman.
Guevara did not stop with the *Dial of Princes*, however. His
other works are also decked out with spurious *humaniores
litterae*, and it is necessary to consider the problem of literary
honesty, to which we will return.

IV *Contemporary Allusions*

There are in the *Dial* more of the oblique references to
contemporary problems. Guevara invents a "most Christian"
king of Africa, Hismaro, and a bishop of Hippo, Silvanus, who,
"desiring to set a good example for their subjects in their
own time and to leave good precepts for future centuries,
convened in the city of Bona a council of all the bishops of
Africa, at which Hismaro himself was present (because in
ancient councils, not only were the kings of the realms present
but also all the lords of high estate) ... I have decided to
place these few [decrees] here so that present-day princes
may see how very Christian the princes of the past were"
(37r). The decrees require provincial councils every two
years; they stipulate that rulers and great lords be present
and that rulers regularly profess the Catholic faith in public.
"We order that the prince have no more than two bishops at

court, one for confession and one to preach the holy Word; and we desire that the council appoint them . . . and that they not remain at court for more than two years, after which two others should replace them . . ." (37r).

Guevara is urging more secular cooperation, particularly as a defense against the spread of heresy among the governing class. Interesting is the rule against more than two bishops in the king's retinue, "because there is nothing more monstrous than to see a church without a prelate for a long time" (*ibid*). Such "absenteeism" was common, even among the lower ranks of the clergy, and the abuses which resulted were often criticized.

The new letter of Marcus to his nephew and its introduction (book I, chapters 41–42) must have been of great consolation to Charles, who was exceptionally homely. He was small and had the Hapsburgs' deformed jaw, which prevented his closing his mouth. This is apparent in all the official portraits, where it is attenuated as much as possible. In old age, with his beard and severe black suits, he became extremely distinguished-looking—if one can believe Titian's marvelous portraits—but as a youth, his gaping mouth was the subject of a number of Spanish jokes. Guevara discovers that the Roman Caesar was ill-proportioned and disreputable in his dress; Hannibal was small, ugly, one-eyed, beetle-browed, and slightly lame; Alexander was small, large-headed, and swarthy. "Good looks and beauty," on the other hand, "are the mother of many vices and the stepmother of all virtues" (43r).

There are many brief passages which seem to have current application: a reference to an imminent fall of Rome because of her wickedness (II, chapter 31); the demoralization and havoc caused by armies and preparations for war (III, chapters 14–16); the "Asiatic" luxuries introduced as a result of foreign wars, such as restaurants, picnics, female actors who dress as men, perfume, etc.; the increased social importance of wealth (III, chapter 25); gaudy displays and frivolous amusements (III, chapter 42); the popularity of actors and jesters (III, chapters 42–47); numerous references to piracy, and so on.

Guevara and his readers believed in the eternal applicability of history. It not only "occurs," but it reenacts eternal patterns or foreshadows them: God punished the desecrators of his temple in pre-Christian times, he destroyed persecutors of his church in early Christian times, and he will soon crush the heretics who have risen in northern Europe. Within the great cycles of history, smaller, personal cycles occur, and man may learn from these how to avoid the snares of fortune. In creating history, Guevara often enhances the "objective" history of antiquity by inserting details which seem visionary, like Cornelia's prophesy of the fall of Rome. It did, of course, fall to the barbarians; but as the reader knew, Rome never seemed to learn her lesson, and she had recently been sacked by Spanish troops— as the wages of iniquity, according to the defenders of Spanish policy. It is now difficult to identify and explain all of these allusions, but they undoubtedly added to the pleasure of the sixteenth-century reader, who could nod his head wisely and think, "How true, how true."

CHAPTER 4

The Lives of Ten Emperors

AS a newly created bishop Guevara must have been a very active man. Not only did he find time to preach at court, work on the royal chronicle (now lost), attend to his ecclesiastical duties, and take part in the expedition to North Africa and Italy, but he managed to write five sizable works which were all published in 1539, only ten years after the *Dial of Princes*. He had already accumulated much of the material for these works during the composition of the *Dial*. He uses the same historical materials in the "compilation" of his *Una década de Césares* (translated into English as *A Chronicle of the Lives of Ten Emperors*); and he mentions in the prologue of the *Dial* that he had planned to write a section on the prince and his courtiers but had left off at the urging of friends anxious to see the first three books of the *Dial* in print. His *The Favored Courtier* (*Aviso de privados*) and *Dispraise of the Life of a Courtier* (*Menosprecio de corte . . .*) are undoubtedly developments of this unfinished portion of the *Dial*. Many of the letters and speeches from *The Familiar Letters* (part I, 1539; part II, 1541) deal with the rebellion of the communes or are addressed to persons who had died some years before, though there is a question whether subject matter is reliable in fixing the date of composition. In any case, the only work begun after 1536 is the *Art of Navigation*.

The evidence that the *Ten Emperors* is his second book comes from the argument of *The Favored Courtier*, where Guevara refers to "the book which we compiled about the virtuous Marcus Aurelius and . . . the other [or next] one which we translated on the lives of the ten Roman princes and now this one. . . ."[1]

I Contents

The prologue of *Ten Emperors*, addressed to Charles V, is a brief essay on kingcraft which summarizes concisely Guevara's ideas on the subject. It is conveniently indexed with marginal glosses: "There must be greatness and nobility in the prince"; "The good prince must open his door to everyone and show everyone a cheerful expression"; "The prince must know the ills of the republic"; "Only he who is virtuous should be favored by the prince," etc. The bishop encapsulates all in an aphorism attributed to Plato: ". . . for a prince to be good, he should give his heart to the republic, his favors to those who serve him, his intentions to the gods, his love to his friends, his secrets to his favorites, and his time to business."[2]

It is insufficient, however, merely to describe the virtues of some ideal prince. To be effective, the virtues must be seen in concrete examples, "for which reason it is necessary for those of us who deal with princes to show them by example that which we set before them in writing . . ." (67). Hence ". . . I decided to translate, compile, and correct the lives of ten Roman princes, in imitation of Plutarch and Suetonius . . ." (69). "The object for which I have undertaken the immense labor of compiling this book, Sire, is that my pen may say to you what my tongue would not say out of reticence . . ." (70).

The *Ten Emperors*, getting off to a somewhat limping start, takes up the life of Trajan, who was born in Spain. He grew up in Cadiz and studied in the famous schools there. After a relatively uneventful youth, he inherited the empire from Nerva and immediately published a series of new laws intended to make life in Rome more agreeable. On his way to settle a war in Africa, he spent the winter in Sicily, improving the customs of the inhabitants; he then returned to Spain (disembarking in his hometown of Cadiz) where he constructed buildings, bridges, and extended an important highway: ". . . [I know this] not because the writers say it expressly but because of the milestones along that highway which say in their inscriptions that they were put there during the time of Trajan . . . I have many times gone there to examine and read and indeed to measure them . . ." (117). Trajan successfully waged war in England, Dacia, Numidia, the Near East, and would have taken a force to India if it had been possible. He died in Cilicia, where he had gone to quell an uprising. Trajan was a man of notable virtues; he was not envious, suspicious, or greedy; he was, however, proud and lecherous:

"...it is true that he never forced anyone, but on the other hand, since he was persuasive and very generous, he never became interested in anyone who did not eventually comply" (97).

The emperor Hadrian was also of Spanish stock on his mother's side, and he returned to Spain at the age of sixteen to see his ancestral country and to study martial arts. Hadrian's passions were hunting, art, women, and later, oratory, after having been embarrassed by his accent: "As Hadrian thought himself very eloquent, one day he acted in a pastoral farce before the Senate, and many orators who were there laughed not only at what he said but at the low style in which he said it" (145).

The saintly Antoninus Pius, father-in-law of Marcus, is the subject of the third biography. Since his life was devoid of scandal, it is not very interesting, as imperial lives go. Antoninus had all the virtues of an ideal ruler; he never shed human blood and matched Numa "not only in the good government of the republic but even in the purity and righteousness of his life" (217).

Chronologically, Marcus Aurelius should of course come next. He is often mentioned in the biography of Antoninus, as is Faustina, "concerning the life of which two, as it pleased God, I compiled a book entitled *Marcus Aurelius*" (186).

In agreeable contrast with his virtuous predecessors, Commodus, the heir of Marcus Aurelius, led an extremely interesting life: he was cruel, lascivious, handsome, athletic, and mad. His undoing came through a rejected woman, a concubine whom he planned to have assassinated but who found out in time to poison him and then have him strangled by a "beardless, shameless, good-for-nothing" named Narcissus. "This then was the end of the shameful and immoral life of Commodus; and princes who live as he did in this world will have such an end, for the sin of the wicked does not go unpunished, though the punishment is delayed for some time" (265).

The emperor Pertinax got his nickname in the days of his youth when he wandered the streets of his hometown selling firewood from the back of an ass. He declined to haggle: "he was so high-priced and so stubborn that if people refused to give him his first price, he preferred not to sell rather than lower the price a farthing..." (266). Offended by his nickname, "he left

his town humiliated and insulted and began to study reading and
writing; and after he had learned that, he worked at learning
the Greek language and Latin. . . . finally he decided to go to
war and learn the military arts, because it seemed to him that
all he got out of study was a great deal of work and no profit
whatsoever . . ." (266–67). As a result of his successful military
expeditions, governorships, and rising prominence in Roman poli-
tics, the assassins of Commodus asked Pertinax to take the title
of emperor. A group of drunken Praetorians murdered him after
a brief and undistinguished reign, because he had curbed their
activities. The Praetorians then auctioned off the emperorship
to the highest bidder, a rich lawyer named Didius Julianus,
whereupon two Roman armies in the East rebelled, and a general,
Septimius Severus, marched on Rome. The Senate ordered the
death of Didius Julianus in order to avert an attack on Rome and
declared Septimius Severus the new emperor. Severus spent his
reign putting down rivals in Greece and England, pacifying the
empire, and thwarting plots. He died ("from pure chagrin")
while on an expedition in England, unsuccessfully fighting against
the guerrilla tactics of the natives.

The two sons of Septimius Severus inherited the empire, which
they at first planned to divide. But the elder, Bassianus, killed
his brother and began a rampage of murders and treacheries
which make repellent reading. An offended bodyguard assassinated him while he was answering the call of nature by "sewing
him to the earth" with a lance. The machinations of his grand-
mother obtained the empire for Bassianus's illegitimate son
Elagabalus. His career of depravities was cut short by a mob of
soldiers. Elagabalus "was the most willful and vicious emperor
in the history of the Roman empire, because the vices that were
scattered among all were found gathered together in this man"
(468).

The last of the ten emperors, one almost as virtuous as Marcus
Aurelius, is Severus Alexander. Though he was Elagabalus's
cousin, no two persons could have been less alike. Severus Alexander was reared with great care by his mother, who protected
him from evil company and instilled in him respect for wisdom
and industry. Of all the Roman emperors, he was the most respectful of scholars. At his accession, Severus Alexander re-

formed religion, government, the court, and his own activities, all of which had suffered under the depraved rule of Egalabalus. He was a talented poet and musician (and could play the organ, flute, viol, shawm, and trumpet), though after he became emperor, he considered it undignified to play instruments. He had a sort of chapel in which he kept pictures of his heroes, including Jesus and Abraham; indeed, he was very tolerant of Christians and Jews and had even considered adding Christ to the Roman pantheon. He was a model of humility, modesty, frugality, chastity, compassion, justice, gratitude, etc., etc. A group of disaffected soldiers, former supporters of Elagabalus, mutinied and killed Severus when he was only twenty-nine years old, "the Roman prince who was most loved during his lifetime and most mourned after his death" (526).

II *Sources and Models*

The *Ten Emperors* is Guevara's most serious effort at writing history. He lists his sources (with some fictitious items) and models. And it is possible, as a result of his own indications and the research of a number of scholars, to see exactly what the bishop took from his sources and what he adds for effect. Most of the ancient works he consulted are already found among the sources of *The Golden Book*: Cassius Dio, Herodian, and the Scriptores Historiae Augustae, principally, with details from Plutarch's *Apophthegmata*, Eutropius, Philostratus, Suetonius, Vegetius.

Since Guevara follows his sources more closely than in *The Golden Book*, it is also possible to see how ill-prepared he was to read the prose of the Scriptores or of the Latin translations of Dio and Herodian. In many passages where there is nothing to be gained by altering the meaning, Guevara obviously mistranslates. He confuses dates, fails to recognize standard classical names, misapplies adjectives, etc. The surviving examples of his original compositions in Latin are additional proof that he had learned simple Church Latin and that in matters of vocabulary, syntax, and spelling, he did not grasp the differences between the still living Medieval Latin and the dead language that his antiquarian contemporaries were reviving.

Fray Antonio's models in the "compilation" of the *Ten Emperors* were, he tells us, Plutarch and Suetonius. Both of these authors, as well as the actual sources, especially the Scriptores Historiae Augustae and Herodian, wrote with an eye to the moral implications of biography. They consciously sought personalities that would illustrate the instability of fortune; they are full of curiosities, sententious sayings, what C. S. Lewis calls "heroic gossip," and the speeches, decrees, and letters normally composed by ancient authors to add rhetorical variety. Guevara assimilated perfectly the moral point of view and the technique of his models. This, no doubt, explains why his works have appealed to admirers of Plutarch: Lord North, the early translator of Plutarch, englished the *Dial of Princes*; E. Clavier, a late eighteenth-century editor of Amyot's Plutarch, included the French version of the *Ten Emperors* as a supplement to his fine edition.

III   *Contemporary Allusions*

The reader will scarcely be surprised to learn that the *Ten Emperors*, like the two earlier works, is full of hints that the strangely modern "Roman" aberrations and laws are disguises for Spanish problems. Laws concerning marriage among equals, the seclusion of women, luxuries, dishonesty in government, racing, excessive wine-drinking, expensive weddings, beggars, superstitions, doctors, etc., are transparently a means for Guevara to present his ideas. Often the same opinions appear undisguised in other works.

Hadrian's reform of British marriage customs ("in particular, he prohibited a husband's having two wives or a woman's having seven husbands ... " [162]) may refer to Henry VIII's questionable marriages, for the death of Catherine of Aragon in 1536 was fresh in everyone's mind. The source on which the passage is based does not mention bigamy.

The Machiavellian letter of a Persian king, who tells Severus Alexander that kingdoms belong to those who have the courage to seize them, may also be a reference to the 1536 war between Francis I and Charles over the duchy of Milan, where the emperor suffered "the first grave military reverse of his career," to quote Royal Tyler.

In chapter XV of the life of Trajan, Guevara invents an expedition from Rome to North Africa, via Sicily. Like Charles V in 1535, Trajan explores the entire island, shoring up fortifications, correcting abuses, granting favors. Like Charles, he sails on to the African coast near the ruins of Carthage, where pestilence proves to be a worse enemy than the Africans. There are other parallels between the activities of Charles and the good Roman emperors which are a subtle form of flattery.

IV   *Influence*

The *Ten Emperors* is fray Antonio's least imaginative work, and it has been one of the least popular. There are two cases, however, which show that it was not entirely neglected, even in the late eighteenth century. The first is the republication by Clavier of the French translation, already noted. It is curious to find a post-*Encyclopédie* Frenchman publishing anything by Guevara, after Pierre Bayle's splenetic attack. The second is two passages taken from the *Ten Emperors* and added to the 1623 English translation of Pedro Mexía's *The Imperial Historie*. Mexía had made several disapproving references to the *Ten Emperors* in his own chronicle of the Roman emperors, though he does not actually name Guevara, and it is poetic justice that Traheron, the translator, should have added Guevara's apochryphal descriptions of Trajan and the deification of Severus Alexander.

CHAPTER 5

The Favored Courtier

I *Contents*

THE original title of the bishop's guide for courtiers, published in 1539, is *Aviso de privados y doctrina de cortesanos*,[1] which means approximately "a warning for favorites and instructions for courtiers." The word *doctrina* frequently signifies religious instruction (*doctrinal* means "catechism," for example); so the title has humorously pious overtones. (Later editions also used the title *Despertador de cortesanos* [An awakening-bell for courtiers].) The book does in fact fall into two parts; the contents would be more accurately described, however, by reversing the parts of the title. The first section provides instructions for courtiers, the second, advice for the successful.

Guevara prefaces this treatise with an analysis of true friendship, which he finds to be unique among human affections in that it only is wholly dedicated to the unselfish love and comfort of another human; and he professes to feel this noble sentiment for Francisco de los Cobos, the royal secretary, to whom he dedicates the work. He offers his book as a token of friendship, since he is unable to repay Cobos's favors with anything but honest advice and the writer's gift of literary immortality, hoping to be to the secretary what philosophers were to the rulers of ancient times, serving his lord with sound counsels. To this end he has read, reread, pondered, and thought up "a new kind of study" (32), which he hopes will awaken the secretary to the instability of fortune and which will stimulate him to practice virtue; for the only treasure which one can accumulate and take from this world is the merit acquired in time virtuously spent.

In his "argument," Guevara illustrates the fondness of the rulers of the past for the company of learned men. Modern men should follow their example, if possible, especially the nobility, but if they cannot surround themselves with philos-

74

ophers, they can at least read good books, from which they will derive "immense profit: for good reading satisfies the will, sharpens the judgment, stifles idleness, inspires the heart, occupies the time..." (43). "Reading a good book is nothing but listening to some wise man" (44).

As an ex-courtier who has, as he says, not read about it but actually experienced it, Guevara can warn the would-be courtier that he must be prepared to suffer the peculiar conditions of a court that moves from city to city and that is founded on a system of competition that breeds self-interest. The physical discomforts and expense of the ambulatory court are great, but worse is the constant anguish created by uncertainty, envy, and suspicion of one's competition. Indeed court life is a kind of voluntary slavery, since one must constantly suppress his own desires and cater to the whims of those whose favor he needs in order to succeed. Such a life is particularly hard on the poor, genteel courtier who must maintain his status, but who is constantly fearful that his miserable existence may be discovered by visitors from his hometown.

Each time the court moves, the worst problem is created by housing. All available accommodations are requisitioned by the king's *aposentadores* ("billet officers"), who allot them by rank and by favoritism. The courtiers are, naturally, never satisfied with their lodgings and inevitably prefer the showy quarters even if they are less comfortable. The billet officers are venal and often ill-tempered, but one must fawn and pretend not to hear their offensive remarks.

The courtier who wishes to succeed should strive to establish a reputation for personal integrity and for honesty in business dealings: "A good reputation is the first step toward influence at court" (84). He should avoid troublemakers and malcontents, "for it is a kind of betrayal to slander the friends we have and the prince we serve" (85). He must realize that princes are subject to whims and that "at times, princes favor certain courtiers because they are inclined to the same tastes rather than others who suffer hardships for the prince's sake" (86). He must therefore cultivate what the prince likes. He should avoid speaking to the prince too often so as not to appear forward or importunate: "...nothing persuades a prince to love his servants so much as seeing that they serve him faithfully and ask little of him" (88).

Guevara gives the would-be courtier his opinions on dignified behavior, including suggestions for a successful audience with the prince, such as hints on the graceful way to bow or kneel and warnings against fidgeting or grimaces, breath tainted by strong foods or drink, harping on the loyal services of one's family or rebuking the prince for his ingratitude, and complaining or arguing, etc. Many of his rules of polite society are still perfectly valid, though a few provide amusing insights into the ways of sixteenth-century society: "[the courtier] should also strive not to spit and especially not to cough, and if by necessity he is constrained to do either, let him bow his head or turn it somewhat, so that he will not breathe in the prince's face" (90).

The bishop formulates general rules on the cultivation of gravity: "One must also observe that if the prince, in private, should indulge in horseplay or satirical remarks, the courtier may be delighted to see it, but he should not forget himself and participate; because it is permissible for the prince to amuse himself, but it is harmful for the courtier to appear frivolous ...; the proper courtier should show prudence in serious matters and gravity in frivolous matters" (93). But if rowdiness shows a want of good sense, chilly severity is likewise undesirable: "At court there are some that eat at the tables of great lords who, though they are humorlessness itself, insist on being witty at table; and if we laugh with them it is not because of what they say but at the flat way they say it" (95). Courtly skills are, as Guevara says many times, a matter of self-discipline: "It is as necessary for courtiers who desire to gain influence and wealth to accustom their tongues to keep silent as it is to teach their bodies to serve" (93).

The new courtier must as soon as possible learn who wields the power at court and make the acquaintance of these persons, "otherwise, gentlemen will have nothing to do with him and doormen will not let him enter. ..." The most efficient way to insinuate oneself into the good graces of the mighty is to begin at the bottom with the favorites of the favorites. It is useless or dangerous to criticize either the system or abuses—which even the king tolerates, Guevara says with obvious bitterness.

On the subject of visiting: one should wait upon everyone of importance, prelates, gentlemen, favorites, and not omit any because our courtier has associated himself with factions. He must time his visit carefully (avoid mealtimes or gambling parties), gauge the humor of the person visited, space his visits (about once a month is sufficient for purely formal calls), and be sensitive to hints which the person visited may offer as to the acceptability of the visit. Insensitivity to such delicate signs is fatal.

It is a good practice for the courtier to accept invitations to dinner very rarely, for invitations put him under obligation to repay the favor. The courtier who occasionally dines out must mind his manners: he must be neat, drink little, praise the host's cook, and refrain from appearing to know too much about fine wines or elaborate dishes, for a *caballero* should know about horses and weapons, innkeepers and cooks about wine and food.

For the sake of his reputation, the courtier must avoid the playboys, gamblers, and riffraff who will swarm around him when he appears at court. A young man must be especially careful and must strive to establish a reputation for gentleman-liness so that other youths will seek him out for worthy activities and shun his company when they plan something frivolous: "It is not, however, the intention of my pen to persuade him to be sanctimonious, that is, rude to the [other] young men, unfriendly with the gallants, gloomy with those who are happy, and silent with those who are making merry, because it does not contribute to one's success as a courtier if, when others are picking up [tennis] balls to play he opens his book-of-hours to pray" (116).

Guevara explains the etiquette of accompanying an important person to the palace, and the fine points of cap-doffing and its social significance. On love: it is *de rigeur* to have a lady friend, otherwise, one may be considered unmanly. "It is a proper pastime for a man who is young, rich, and unattached to serve a lady at court; but let him who is poor and has no influence refrain from love affairs with ladies or friendships with nuns, because the occupation of the lady is to fleece the man who serves her and that of the nun is to ask favors of the man who visits her. He who offers to serve a lady commits himself to keep very strict vows..." (129).

The serious courtier should attend the king's levee and his meals as often as possible, since it is a courtesy and also provides opportunities for business. The courtier must not touch the king's clothing or tableware, he should avoid bandying words with the court jesters, he should bow profoundly when the king sneezes, etc., and he should practice the kings's favorite sport, such as falconry or hunting, where "the king can hunt prey and the courtier can hunt influence" (132).

There is a special kind of courtier who has not come to court to make his fortune but to start a lawsuit. The bishop, who had much experience in law courts, warns the litigant about the anxieties, the possible losses, the complexity of the law (which is such that even the greatest legal theorists like Plato never wrote anything on litigation), the constant expenditures on lawyers, clerks, and officers, the eccentricities of judges, and the dishonesty of lawyers (who "for the profit of ten doubloons with no qualms attack the truth as well as defend the right") (140).

The second part of the book, "a warning to favorites," is addressed to the courtier who has succeeded in rising to a position of influence at court. The principal virtue for the successful courtier is, once again, patience. He must learn to swallow insults, suppress his anger, maintain strict impartiality, and must refuse to listen to, or be affected by, scurrilous attacks on himself. The higher he rises, the more cautious he must be, since all influence and success is persecuted by envy, and he will be blamed for the prince's faults. Most of all, he must absolutely refuse to take sides in controversies: "the favorites of princes are sooner ruined by the factions that they support than by the favors they request" (149). Before explaining the *privado's* duties, Guevara paints in dark tones the difficulties of the courtier who attempts to transact business or present a petition at court. The principal obstacle to prompt, equitable settlement of such affairs are the junior officials and clerks in the offices of the *privado*; these men live high on bribes, and their offensive manners reflect ill on the reputations of their master.

Chapter XIII is a sermonlike warning against pride, summed up concisely by the chapter heading, "that the favorites of the princes should take care not to be proud, for they never fall from their post except because of this accursed vice." Chapter XIV—also long and dull—is a warning against greed and the ostentation of wealth by favorites. Chapters XV and XVI, "of very notable doctrine," expound the instability of political life at court.

Privados must exert themselves to overcome the human weakness for sexual pleasures, for though concupiscence "is not the gravest of sins, it is the most dangerous for one's reputation" (216). "The servants and favorites of princes must be untainted by immoral relations with women, especially with those who come to them in their official capacity, because it is a great offense against God and a great treason against the king [for these *privados*] to send a woman away with her name disgraced instead of her business dispatched" (221).

After attacking pride and lust, Guevara shows the *privado* the disadvantages of gluttony, which, he says, is the mother of lust. Related to this subject is the problem of costly banquets recently introduced from France, which encourage gluttony, drunkenness, and slanderous conversation, and which leave the *privado* open to influence and bribery. On the dangers of loose talk, gossip, and indiscretion in the *privado*, Guevara warns: "The king's *privado* should esteem the secrets which the prince reveals to him more highly than the boons which [the king] grants to him" (249). He must be especially careful of people who, like terriers, smell out secrets for profit, and of women, who are constitutionally incapable of secrecy.

Following up the observations on unbridled tongues, Guevara passes on to the truthfulness of the *privado*, his most important positive quality: "He who is a friend of truth is a friend of justice, and he who is a friend of justice is a friend of the state . . ." (265).

II   *Sources*

Alvarez de la Villa, the most recent editor of *The Favored Courtier*, has suggested that Guevara's inspiration for it is Baldesar Castiglione's *Book of the Courtier*, one of the most widely read and admired works of the early sixteenth century. No doubt Guevara had read it. Castiglione was Papal Nuncio in Spain from 1525 until his death in 1529 (a few days after his confirmation as bishop of Avila); he made the final corrections on his manuscript of the *Courtier* in Spain and added a number of references to Spanish matters; and half of the first Aldine edition was sent to Castiglione in Spain, including a sumptuous vellum copy for the emperor. The success of the work was so great that new editions appeared immediately. In 1534 Juan Boscán made his brilliant Spanish translation, the first into any foreign language.

Guevara almost certainly knew Castiglione; both were with the court in 1527 and 1528, during which time Guevara received the miter. Castiglione must have heard Guevara preach, and he surely heard the splendid speech which Guevara wrote for Charles V for delivery in September 1528, announcing his plans to go to Italy to receive the Imperial Crown. It is therefore reasonable to assume that Guevara knew both Castiglione and his work. Even if we should learn, however, that Guevara had never set eyes on either, it is still also reasonable to assume that so influential a work should at least have some indirect effect on the contents of Guevara's *Favored Courtier*.[2] But, in fact, there are no obvious traces, though there are a number of parallels, first because both were writing about the same sort of person, the courtier, and second, because their educations were naturally very similar, as a comparison of the sources of anecdotes in the *Courtier* and the *Dial* plainly shows. But Castiglione was using his charming imitation of a Platonic dialogue to create an ideal courtier, whose highest purpose was to educate the prince whom he served, whereas Guevara's principal object is, I should say, the moral instruction of high officials, though the doctrinal portion of the *Favored Courtier* occupies only the final chapters. It is in some ways a negative approach to what Castiglione had tried to do in a positive way: Castiglione's courtier is formed by the accumulation of courtly virtues; the *privado* is perfected by the correction of defects or weaknesses; he is advised to curb his emotions, to remind himself constantly that nothing endures. Guevara's approach is, logically enough, that of a trained preacher, who develops his thought by means of themes, *exempla*, and perorations, and it has the charm of Guevara's best Sunday style, with his farfetched anecdotes and personal remembrances.

The similarities between the *Courtier*, II. 18–20, and the *Favored Courtier*, chapters IV and V, are sufficiently striking to suggest that Guevara examined Castiglione before composing these pages of his treatise. Both authors advise the aspiring courtier to find out what their lords like and then cultivate it; to avoid creating situations which are unpleasant for the lord, such as asking for inappropriate favors; to adjust themselves to the lords' humor; to estimate their own talents for banter and joking and not try to be funny if they are not naturally humorous. These parallels and a few others make it conceivable that Guevara took material from Castiglione; but any sixteenth-century writer of precepts for courtiers would surely have used most of these arguments, and it is only the fact that a number of similar ones are clustered in this portion of the *Favored Courtier* that suggests Castiglione's works as the immediate source.

The main source is, as Guevara states, his own experiences at court and—as we shall see in a moment in the discussion of contemporary allusions—the abuses which he saw all about him. The anecdotes from the lives of philosophers and the learned references are, of course, mainly fiction, though no one has yet taken the trouble to study them.

One section of the *Favored Courtier* which is more seriously "historical" and less personal and which therefore may have a literary source is chapter XVIII, on banquets. It begins as a tirade against gluttony, the mother of the other sins, contrasting the depravity of modern society and the wholesomeness of the ancient Golden Age. Guevara records an anecdote in which Plato expresses his horror at the gluttony of Dionysius of Syracuse, who not only ate dinner *but also supper.* Modern man not only refuses to be content with one meal a day but insists on unhealthy variety and spices. It is possible to show, says Guevara, that the devil is always present at banquets: for example, Adam's apple, Esau's mess of potage, Belshazzar's feast, etc., etc. And he reviews sumptuary laws which he claims to have taken from Macrobius and Aulus Gellius (235).

The ill effects of banqueting are sluggishness and dulled

judgment—both great defects in a *privado* who must conduct
the affairs of the state; the bad example and excuse for slander
and envy; harmful gossip that invariably arises from chatter
at banquets ("afterward, they do not say what the *privado* said
but what they think he meant to say, so that there are not so
many glosses on the Bible as there are opinions about some
remark that they heard and the *privado* made at table" [238]);
and the obligation that such banquets impose on the guests.

The principal inspiration for this chapter is John of Salisbury's
Policraticus, book VIII, chapters 6–7, on gluttony and banqueting.
Guevara follows John's line of argument, amplifying and chang-
ing as usual. John's seventh chapter discusses Roman sumptuary
laws, but Guevara here changes (pp. 223 ff.) to Aulus Gellius
(II. 24) as a source for his own account of these laws.

The best place to see the literary sources which contain the
kinds of ideas (many perfectly commonplace in the sixteenth
century) that Guevara was amplifying is Pedro Mexía's "Two
Dialogues on Banqueting" ("Los dos coloquios del combite"),
published in 1547 by Guevara's successor in the office of
chronicler. The excellent edition by Dr. Margaret L. Mulroney
(Iowa, 1930) provides notes on the sources, many of which
are identified by Mexía himself. It seems to me possible that
Mexía was stimulated to write these dialogues as a way of
showing up and correcting Guevara's unscholarly treatment of
a serious subject. One of the interlocutors in this delightful
little work is "a learned man called Master Velázquez"—master
being the title used for clergymen which Guevara applied to
himself on a number of occasions—who is reluctant to accept
an invitation to a banquet because of the prescriptions against
them by various Fathers such as Jerome and Gregory, whom
he cites. Other speakers contradict the *maestro* and prove to
him that not only can banquets be shown by passages from the
Scriptures to be good things but also by passages from the
ancients, such as Plato, Cicero, Plutarch, and the like. Plutarch
quotes Paulus Emilius as saying that splendid banquets were
in fact suitable to noble spirits because they intimidated one's
enemies and won friends. Maestro Velázquez declares that he
is in reality already convinced that banquets are fine things
under the proper circumstances and that what he has said

applied to "the excesses that one sees at banquets these days" (60). The dialogue then ranges through costly feasts among the ancients, the ideal number of guests, whether the ancients ate only once a day (65) as many believe, whether variety is harmful, etc.

There is no allusion to Guevara, unless it is so subtle as to be unrecognizable; but the work is a compendium of remarks on banqueting and eating from ancient writers, the church fathers, and moderns (like Budé and Vives), and it provides a corrective to the uniformly unfavorable picture of banquets which Guevara had painted. Mexía was too good a humanist to allow so "classical" an institution as the *symposium* to go undefended. To judge from Mexía's citations, Guevara's ideas were colored by his monastic education and readings from Gregory (*Nulla pene conviva sine culpa, propter voluptatem et loquacitatem* [56, note. 5]), Jerome (*Conviva tibi vitanda sunt saecularium* [58, note 15]), and no doubt their commentators. It is unlikely that a more immediate source is to be found for these pages in Guevara.

III *Contemporary References: Guevara and Cobos*

Guevara dedicated his *Favored Courtier,* as well as the *Art of Navigation,* to Charles's Castilian secretary, Francisco de los Cobos, Grand Commander (*Comendador mayor*) of Leon in the order of St. James and member of the Council of State. Cobos has been (until Hayward Keniston's fine biography appeared)[3] one of the least appreciated figures of Charles's administration, though he was in fact the single most important government officer for Castilian affairs for about twenty years. When Guevara wrote his dedicatory epistle in the late 1530s, Cobos was, in Keniston's words, the "elder statesman" of Charles's Spanish administration, and his rise to power and immense wealth is a remarkable success story.

By a combination of extraordinary charm, unfailing loyalty to his master and to his friends, and diligence, he had become the director of almost all government business by the early 1520s. He accumulated a large number of salaried posts for himself and his family, received gifts from the emperor and from favor-seekers, and eventually rose as high in society as was possible for an untitled gentleman, with one of the two *encomiendas mayores* ("grand commanderies") in the great military order. By purchasing a number of properties from the military orders, he was also able to add the style Lord of Sabiote, etc., to his name. His power and riches brought him an aristocratic bride, a duke for a son-in-law, and eventually a marquisate for his own son. (The present duchess of Alcalá is his direct descendant.)

In the preface of the *Favored Courtier*, addressed to Cobos, Guevara suggests in ambiguous language (like that, e.g., on p. 26), which may be taken either as the usual obsequious commonplaces of dedication or as the familiar address of an old friend, that he is offering Cobos the work in a spirit of frank criticism, because high officials hear only flattery (28, 50). He never, however, hints that the vices that he hopes to correct by means of his book are those of Cobos rather than universal human weaknesses or universally tolerated practices. It is perfectly arguable, therefore, that Guevara, as a moralist, is doing what all preachers do, namely, criticizing prevalent abuses, and that in fact those which he singles out are practically eternal and are to be found in Spanish moralistic writing since at least the days of Pero López de Ayala. I think, however, that it is quite as possible to say that Guevara selected these very abuses with the addressee, Cobos, in mind, and that he pushes his criticisms daringly close to personal criticism. We have no idea what gossip about Cobos's affairs was current when Guevara was writing, how really close Guevara was to the *privado*, and how flamboyant the *privado*'s life style may have looked when compared to that of the other rich courtiers who vied for status by displaying their riches. But I think we are safe in believing that the bishop is discussing real abuses—disguising them with some discretion, naturally—which he thinks the *privado* must seek to correct. Those precepts which appear to me most likely to allude to Cobos are the following:

1. Guevara stresses that the *privado* must avoid siding with rival factions at court. Cobos was apparently a good example of a court official who managed to straddle the fence with great skill. In a secret memorandum written by Charles V to

Philip, he notes that Cobos has up to that point (1543) managed to avoid aligning himself, though he feels that Cobos's wife "is responsible for involving him in rivalries" (Keniston, p. 258).

2. Guevara rails at the bribery allowed in government offices and warns the *privado* that he must supervise his clerks as closely as a prelate supervises his monks: "Princes are satisfied if we obey them; *privados* are satisfied if we serve them; but their servants are not content unless we worship them" (156). "In my presence a petitioner from Cordoba once gave an accounting official eight *reales* for dispatching a certain business, which [money the official] refused to take, and when [the petitioner] swore and swore that he had only four *reales* left for his journey home and begged me to urge [the officer] to accept them, he said to us, "Look gentlemen, ... I swear by Our Lady of Guadalupe that it has been more than two years since I accepted a silver coin or had anything in my hands but a gold-piece" (158). Such abuses may occur, says Guevara, but they will eventually disgrace the man in whose service the dishonest clerk works.

3. In his warnings to the *privado* against the sin of pride, Guevara seems to tread on dangerous ground with his examples of the lowly who have risen to great heights. Cobos was, according to Keniston's evidence (68), very desirous of social status, and he went to unbelievable lengths to insure that his posterity would have the money and titles that he had been denied. Such actions as remodeling his family home into a palace, buying castles in nearby towns, and so on suggest that he might not have liked to be reminded that in his youth he hawked the lace caps that his sisters knitted—or so it was said.

Guevara recounts the example of Agathocles, a potter's son who became king of Sicily, who always ate from earthenware dishes to remind himself of his humble origins: "It may be that the *privado* before he rose to become *privado*, was a person of not very good lineage, from a not very exalted homeland, not very gifted and not very favored by fortune; [yet the *privado*] should not only not be affronted by all of these things but should even be proud, because at court, people will hold him in higher esteem for taking pride in what he was before than they will esteem him for growing proud of what he is now" (171).

Guevara also warns the hypothetical *privado* not to quibble over precedence in court ceremonies, the clear inference being that many of the courtiers will be of better lineage and therefore would take precedence: "it means nothing for someone to take the lead in mounting the staircase of stone, since he has left everyone behind when he mounted the staircase of favor" (174).

4. Fray Antonio again verges on the tactless in his discussion of the evil effects of avarice and of conspicuous luxuries: "Let the *privados* take care not to make a show of wealth in public, but if they have a little something left over, let them keep it secret, because if their enemies do not know what they have, they can only slander them, but if they see it, they will not fail to accuse them. They see a courtier build proud buildings, line his house with monstrous tapestries, waste a great deal of food in his pantry, adorn his sideboard with very rich vessels; they see rich presents pouring in; [the courtier] is reputed to be very rich and goes about accompanied by many servants—all this is not only always a cause of gossip but, at the right time and in the right place, a cause of criticism and accusation" (185).

By only 1524, Cobos was so rich that he could remodel and enlarge houses that he had received as part of his wife's dowry. He continued to ornament his palace until it was the most sumptuous in Valladolid—the emperor described it as "imperial"—and suitable to house the royal family. The tapestries and tableware which Guevara mentions were standard equipment in rich households of the sixteenth century, but Cobos's possessions were so exceptional that he himself entailed in an estate for his son such things as his gold and scarlet bed, wall hangings of cloth-of-gold and crimson, and tapestries of the *Triumphs* of Petrarch; and among the treasures auctioned at his death were thirty-one platters and vessels of gold "as valuable as any the Emperor might have" (quoted by Keniston, p. 318).

5. The bishop's observations on illicit sexual relations (not the gravest of sins but the most harmful to one's good name [216]), recall Cobos's reputation for womanizing: the emperor, for example, warned Philip II that Cobos had a weakness for women

and would encourage it in Philip if he got the chance (Keniston, p. 259). Early in 1538, one of Cobos's servants wrote to another that the secretary was behaving disgracefully with regard to women and that there might be undesirable consequences. We can take Guevara's word that many women sought to obtain government favors by offering their own favors to those in influential positions.

6. Though there is only indirect evidence for it, Cobos's palace must have been the scene of a great deal of banqueting. Keniston mentions one extravagant affair which took place at the marriage of his daughter to the duke of Sessa in 1541 (and therefore after the publication of the *Favored Courtier*). But descriptions of this banquet and the inventories of auctions after Cobos's death show plainly that his household was equipped with a great deal of the most lavish tablesettings—gold and silver vessels and cloth-of-silver table linens—so we may safely assume that Guevara had Cobos's own banquets in mind when he rails against the expense, the waste, and the unhealthiness of banqueting.

IV   *Influence: The Picaresque Novel*

Guevara describes the humiliations and sufferings of the poor gentlemen who live at court, in dread that someone will discover their shame: "His heart suffers more from revealing his poverty and misery than it suffers from enduring it . . ." (57). "A courtier and his servant-boy get by with only a meat pie for supper or some sheep's-trotters, and sometimes they get by with only radishes and cheese . . . Without comparison men spend more to comply with those who see them than to satisfy their desires. The courtier who is honorable and well bred prefers to fast rather than to give anyone matter for gossip" (58). The poor courtier is constantly in debt and in fear of having his possessions impounded. He must dress well, whether he can afford it or not: "Once he makes up his mind to go about the court, he must appear very well dressed or not consider himself a courtier, because in this case poverty is not counted as an excuse, but people ascribe it to stinginess or infamy" (121).

Among other precepts that Guevara repeats several times is one to the effect that a polite courtier never shows his hard

feelings by refusing to speak to his enemies or to doff his cap:
"those who are of a low sort show their enmities by refusing
to speak" (98). "A proper courtier should speak to whoever
speaks to him, bow to whoever bows to him, and doff his cap
to whoever doffs his cap, without regard to whether the other
is his friend or his enemy, because it is a matter of breeding....
It is more characteristic of plebeians than of gentlemen who
desire to show their dislikes in such low ways..." (127).

To every literate Spaniard, the mere mention of the penniless
courtier who makes a show of prosperity suggests the poor
squire of *Lazarillo de Tormes*, published in 1557. Other passages
in Guevara's work likewise call to mind the squire, who, it will
be remembered, leaves his hometown in order to avoid raising
his cap to a rich gentleman, because the gentleman in question
never raises his cap *first*. The touchy squire, who has abandoned
his ruinous estates in Old Castile just to preserve his "honor,"
tells Lazarillo how he himself had insulted and almost struck
a workman who had addressed him with "God keep your
worship" instead of removing his cap and saying "I kiss you
worship's hands."

The squire, who for all his charm suffers from the worst kind
of false pride, is looking for some great lord who will pay well
for his services.

But do I not have the talent to serve and content one of these [lords]?
By God, if I should ever find him, I would be his *privado*, and I
would do him a thousand services, because I would know how to
lie to him as well as another and to please him to perfection. I would
laugh at his witticisms and his actions, even if they were not the
best in the world. I would never tell him anything that annoyed him,
even if it were greatly to his benefit. I would be very diligent to
serve him in word and deed. I wouldn't kill myself doing things that
he wouldn't see.... I would praise what he liked and on the other
hand slander, scoff at, and inform on members of the household and
outsiders, investigate and try to find out other people's affairs in
order to tell them to him, and many other accomplishments of this
sort which are found in noble households these days and which the
lords like. They don't want to see virtuous men in their houses; on the
contrary, they loathe them and despise them and call them fools
and say they are undependable or that they are not persons with

whom the lord can relax. And with these [lords], clever men behave these days as I would behave, but my bad luck keeps me from finding him.

This passage from *Lazarillo* is a perfect perversion of what Guevara (and Castiglione) had set before their readers, and its humor depends on one's familiarity with the ideal that it parodies. It is difficult to tell how widely read Guevara's work may have been, but in any case it embodies the moralists' concept of the faithful servant which the anonymous author of *Lazarillo* is satirizing. Angel del Río (*Historia de la literatura española*, I, 168) says, without mentioning this work, that the bishop's writings "had a great influence on Spanish literature, visible in the picaresque" and other genres. And Angel Valbuena Prat (in *La novela picaresca española*, 5th ed., p. 34) observes that the author of *Lazarillo* used not only folk material but motifs which appeared in the literature of the period, such as the poor squire in an *auto* ("farce") of Gil Vicente or a needy gentleman described by Guevara in one of his epistles. There are in fact many such references in the works of Guevara, but perhaps these in the *Favored Courtier* are the most pertinent to the evaluation of possible influence of Guevara on *Lazarillo*. It seems likely to me that Guevara's contemporaries read him more for his satire than we tend to think.

Another suggestive point of contact between Guevara and the picaresque is Guevara's mild warning against courting nuns— if you are poor—because they constantly beg for things. The platonic courtship of nuns was apparently quite common, to judge from a passage in Quevedo's *Buscón*, where the author satirizes the lovers of nuns and the extraordinary inconveniences which the natural restrictions of their ladies' profession placed upon conversation.

I see no reason to suppose that Quevedo got his idea from Guevara, but I think it worth while to point out that Quevedo confirms this curious social practice of the upper classes observed by Guevara. Though the *Buscón* appeared almost three quarters of a century later, it is the only other supporting document I know of from the Golden Age. And it is curious that neither Guevara nor Quevedo condemn the courting of nuns

on religious grounds but only because of its inconveniences
(Guevara) or the inherent foolishness of the situation (Quevedo).

I have also observed a few allusions to Guevara in Mateo
Luján's continuation of *Guzmán de Alfarache*, which I shall
record here as another bit of evidence of the "classic" status
of Guevara's writings in the seventeenth century: In book II,
chapter V, Guzmán goes to Alcalá de Henares to pursue his
studies. When his seedy appearance repels a group of new
students, who order him to eat in the kitchen, Guzmán delivers
an oration, bristling with Latin, on the danger of judging by
appearances, comparing himself to the *villano del Danubio*. In
addition to this allusion, Luján in many places of his work
plays with scholarly material, interlarding references to real
but obscure works or persons with fictional ones, as Guevara
does (e.g., book I, chapter III).

CHAPTER 6

A Dispraise of the Courtier's Life

A Dispraise of the Courtier's Life and a Commendation of the Life of the Laboring Man is the unwieldy title under which the first English translation of *Menosprecio de corte y alabanza de aldea* appeared in 1548, nine years after the publication of the Spanish original. The Spanish title really translates as "Criticism of the city and praise of the village," with the additional connotations of *menosprecio* ("scorning, spurning, rejection") and *corte* ("court, capital, city"). The *Dispraise*[1] (for short) has been one of Guevara's most popular works. It is clearly from the same vein as the *Dial* and the *Favored Courtier*, both of which are echoed in many passages, and I am inclined to think of it as a continuation of the *Favored Courtier*.

I Contents

In the prologue, Guevara offers the work to King John III of Portugal as the best service he can perform: "he who gives good advice to his prince and lord does him a much greater good than he who performs for him some notable service" (16). But Guevara sees his own folly in telling others, especially a great ruler, how to lead his life well, when he himself has failed so miserably: "I confess, your serene highness, that I have fallen —stumbled, and indeed landed face down—into all of the things which I describe and criticize in this, your book; for though I am the least of courtiers, I am the greatest of sinners" (8–9). "...And since one cannot understand this work well if he does not know about the author of it, the course of his life will be told in a few words, so that those who read this writing will know how the world has taken all the flour and scarcely left the bran for Christ" (9–10). Guevara tells of his "vicious" childhood, entrance into a monastery, summons from the emperor, and

91

travels. "I have given this account to your highness, most exalted
prince, so that you may know that all that I shall say in this, your
book, this your servant has not dreamed or discovered by asking
but has seen with his eyes, walked with his feet, touched with
his hands, and indeed mourned in his heart; one should believe
him, therefore, as a man who has seen what he writes and experienced what he says" (11).

In the first two chapters Guevara states that each man is
responsible for his own actions and that a sensible man learns
to be wary of life's deceptions and of his own sensuality. Each
man must consider his inclinations and choose the estate that
lets him live honestly and die a Christian death. He may find
that a courtier's life is unsuitable for him. The man who decides
to leave the court should begin to prepare himself mentally,
study his own weaknesses, and attack them one at a time. It is
difficult to eradicate habits and thoughts; even in the solitude
of his house, his heart will beat faster when he hears of new
vacancies to be filled. Once he has retired, the ex-courtier must
find useful occupation; "No one should think, because he has
come to live in the village and has retired to his home, that therefore necessity is not going to seek him out and annoyances are
not going to find him" (62). He must make a positive effort to
keep busy, to find interesting company and good books, to get on
with his neighbors (though avoiding even modest local honors
such as a mayoralty: "the affairs of a village are annoying and
costly" [63]), to live frugally, to support charities, fulfill religious
duties ("virtuous exercises, although they are tiring at first,
eventually bring pleasure" [65]), and to distribute his wealth.
"Let no one say that all of the aforesaid things are hard to fulfill,
though they are easy to read; because if we want to exert ourselves, we are capable of much more than we realize" (66).

Village life is free of problems which plague the wandering
court, the worst of which is housing. Life in a small town is relatively free of competition for status. A simple gentleman or a
well-to-do villager is someone important; at court, he is a nobody.
Village dwellers have time for innocent pleasures and religious
duties; courtiers spend their time in litigations, attempting to influence officials, and swindling one another. Villagers act and
dress as they please; courtiers can never relax the constraining

etiquette which the relentless hunt for status forces upon them. Consider the poor *hidalgo*, going to market:

> In wintertime he wears a long hooded cloak, he wraps a homely scarf about his head, he pulls an old hat down around his ears, he puts on riding spurs, he shoes himself in his Sunday shoes, he rents a she-donkey from his neighbor, he goes off mounted on her with his feet in the saddlebags, carying a stick to prod her with; and best of all, he tells those he meets that his horse stepped on a nail, and those at the market that his horse is tied up at the inn near the bridge. When he returns to the village, he tells his neighbors that he went to the city to visit a sick friend or to plead for someone in jail or to present a lawsuit or to set a price on a colt or to buy silk and woolen cloth or to collect a third of his salary, when the truth is that his saddlebags are full of herbs for the pot, salt for the house, shoes for the household, oil for Friday, lamps to light the dinner table, and perhaps even a pruning hook for pruning his vineyard. I beg those who read this writing not to laugh at what we have said but to take note: for it is sounder advice for a poor *hidalgo* to seek something to eat on a donkey than to ride a horse and starve. (76–77)

Village life is also healthier. Food is good and cheap, firewood is plentiful, and amusements and exercises are wholesome. In the capital, food is bad and costly, meals are often disagreeable because of the company, firewood is scarce, and the tall buildings and gloomy streets "corrupt" the air.

Most courtiers are so perverse, however, that they prefer the hardships of life at the center of activity. If he must return to his village, he has only contempt for the village clods. "But if we examine what he does and the good breeding that he brings from court, [we see that] it is to go to bed at midnight, to get up at eleven, to dress very slowly, wear close-fitting hose, lace himself tightly, comb his hair often, insist on wearing a cap constantly, talk about the mistress he had at court, stroke his beard when he speaks, tell a thousand lies about the war, borrow money from the priest, court some little married woman, and spend the day wandering through the village with a walking stick" (144).

In contrast to the decadence of modern courts, chroniclers of earlier times record the virtue to be found in the courts and cities of antiquity: their abundance, wealth, discipline, learning, chastity, industry, abstemiousness, indifference to wealth, etc. What a sad decline: "How shall we praise our century for men illustrious in arms and learned in the sciences, when strength is used for robbing and learning for deceiving? . . . How can we praise our century for the great amount of study and the small amount of idle talk, when most of the students in the universities only learn to gossip and to write verses and farces? . . . How can we praise our century for not being covetous or avaricious, when not only do men not throw gold and silver into the sea [as the ancient dwellers of the Balearic islands did] but even go to the Indies in search of it?" (158–59).

Many famous men of antiquity, "moved by sheer goodness and of their own will, [left court and] went to set their lives in order before death should waylay them" (173). An example is Pericles, who retired from governing Athens and went to a village, where he lived fifteen years, plowing by day and reading by night. Great men of antiquity like Pericles left court out of a desire to prepare for death, and not because they were poor, ashamed, deprived, or exiled. Guevara himself is an example of the modern courtier who has been seduced by life at court and tainted by its evils. "Oh how often was I seized with a desire to retire from court, to withdraw from the world, to become a hermit or a Carthusian monk; but I did not desire this because I was virtuous but because I was desperate, because the king did not give me what I wanted, and the favorite refused to see me" (180).

Even now, says the bishop, when his friends are dead, his strength failing, his pleasures losing their attractions, even now, his heart betrays his good intentions and he finds himself still interested in worldly matters, still resentful of slights, still prone to talk too much. "Behold, then, how I have spent my boyhood, wasted my youth, and used my old age; and the worst is that I have not known how to benefit myself or use the time well or recognize opportunity, or even enjoy the court; because I finally know it for what it is when it is time to leave it" (187). And he takes leave of worldly concerns with a grave litany of the world's deceptions, punctuated with the phrase, repeated like a response, Quédate adios, Mundo, "Goodbye, world."[2]

II *Sources*

M. Martínez de Burgos, editor of the standard text of the *Dispraise*, believes that Guevara "was indebted only to his fertile wit and to his personal experience" for the idea and form of the book, though the bishop made use of his favorite authors—principally Plutarch, Diogenes Laertius, and the Roman historians—for the erudition which ornamented all serious work of the sixteenth century. (He lists these general sources on pp. XIX and XX and includes passages from Rúa's letters exposing Guevara's fictions and errors in footnotes.)

Whatever Guevara's original inspiration, "the miseries of the courtier" had been a popular theme for moralists and satirists since the Middle Ages. Much of what Pauline M. Smith says in her excellent study, *The Anti-Courtier Trend in Sixteenth Century French Literature*, applies to Spanish. Her account of the classical, medieval, Neo-Latin, and Italian models is so thorough that I shall merely add a few examples which illustrate the "availability" of the theme to Guevara in the early sixteenth century. Dr. Smith sees "the influence of Horace and Claudian in Guevara's constantly recurring formula *o bienaventurado* ['Fortunate is he . . .'] in the early chapters, the equivalent of *beatus ille* and *felix qui*. But Guevara's development of the theme of the delights of country life has far less charm than Horace's and points perhaps in addition to the inspiration of a more ascetic author, namely Seneca. Guevara's ideas on the purpose of retirement, that it should be considered as an opportunity for moral self-improvement through virtuous pursuits, this idea is fundamental to Seneca as well" (Smith, p. 35).

The most famous medieval disparagers of court life are John of Salisbury, from whose *Policratus* Guevara had used material in the *Favored Courtier*, and Petrarch. Among Guevara's contemporaries Castiglione's *Courtier* provoked adverse reactions to his idealized picture of court life—one of these reactions being Guevara's own work, according to Dr. Smith—and the plays and virulent dialogues of Pietro Aretino found imitators in the later sixteenth century.

In Spain itself, Guevara's only predecessor seems to have been the great statesman and author Pero López de Ayala (1332–

1407). One of Chancellor López de Ayala's best-known works is a long poem—or group of poems—the *Rimado de palacio* (Rhymed Book of the Palace), that is to say, "A poem about Court," though it contains a great deal besides poetry about court life. In quatrains 422–75, a section subtitled "Los fechos de palacio" (Happenings at court), the chancellor of Castile describes in the first person his experiences: "I have wasted a great part of my life / serving earthly lords with great diligence; / now I see and am beginning to understand / that the more one labors there, the more he will lose. / Who can imagine what the courts of kings are like? / How much misfortune and travail a man must suffer! / [He risks] dangers in his body and damnation for his soul. . . ." Pero López tells how he returned to court from a journey only to find his party in disfavor, new servants who refuse to let him enter the palace or who demand bribes; the king is cold to him; his salary unpaid for three months. The favorite and the king's accountants, in collusion, bilk him out of his expensive mule and some fine cloth, and give him a bill of exchange addressed to a treasurer who claims that he does not have the money in question; Pero López finally must borrow money from a Jewish lender.

When he describes the difficult life of the king, he also touches upon the disorderly, litigious, bloodthirsty, greedy courtiers who surround the ruler (quatrains 476–518). And in a section (quatrains 476–518) which is a minature *Aviso de privados,* he gives examples of favorites who have fallen because of their greed. Like fray Antonio, Pero López advises the man who has risen to importance at court to retire voluntarily before fortune topples him (quatrains 670–671).

Around the time that the *Canciller* was writing the poem on his disillusionments at court, the greatest scholar of the day, Francesco Petrarca (1303–1374) wrote a treatise on the life of solitude (*De vita solitaria*) which celebrates "the beauty of a life of leisure, retired from crowded haunts and importunate cares" (55) in a "highly rhetorical antithesis between the joys of the peaceful recluse and the cares of the busy worldling."[3] Petrarch's subject is not a courtier but an Italian *bourgeois,* though the differences are not great.

The similarities between the *Dispraise* and the *Life of Solitude*

I take to be due to their sources, which include not only Horace, but the whole Western tradition of philosophy and theology which praises simplicity and frugality, and which makes them religious virtues, as opposed to wealth or power and the organized vices of city life: for example, Petrarch urges each man "seriously to take into account the disposition with which nature has endowed him" before deciding on a way of life, since the solitary life of self-realization will not suit everyone (see *Dispraise*, pp. 38–40).

One of the most famous examples of the *Dispraise* theme, certainly available to Guevara, is Pope Pius II's *De Miseriis Curialium*, written in the 1440s and in print from about 1470. It was translated into Spanish in 1520 by Archdeacon Diego López. The little treatise, in the form of a letter, "gives a list of the various objects for which most men resort to court—honor, fame, power, riches or pleasure ... Then it argues in detail that all these classes are doomed in advance to disappointment. ... Finally he writes of the few noble souls who devote themselves to the court for worthy motives—to do some patriotic service, or improve their minds by lofty intercourse. But these also find no pleasure or profit there. They have miserable lodgings, and coarse irregular meals. They have no liberty of thought or action, no place or leisure for study, no chance of learning good morals or manners, no way of making true friends. They get only a scanty pay, and have great difficulty in collecting even that. And when they reflect on their way of life, they are tortured by their conscience."[4] Thus Professor Mustard summarizes the contents of the treatise, which was also paraphrased by Alexander Barclay in the "earliest English eclogues," the *Miseryes of Courtiers and Courts of Princes in general.* The great number of similarities of thought between Guevara's *Dispraise* and Pius II's letter, though I find only questionable verbal coincidences, show plainly that the ideas—some of which come from so ancient a source as Juvenal— were common intellectual property, that they were in a technical sense the commonplaces of moral rhetoric. Even such seemingly realistic sections of *De Miseriis* as 18–27, which contrast the bad food and drink found at court with the pleasant meal of the private citizen, are derived from Juvenal or Seneca. Guevara, who also devotes a good deal of space to the poor cuisine at court, extends the other pole of the comparison and describes in detail the gustatory delights of the country (and for his pains brings down the wrath of María Rosa Lida on his head).[5] But in these passages, I find no evidence that Guevara had *De Miseriis* in mind; the striking resemblances are merely another example of the uniformity of European culture in the sixteenth century.

Even the pose of the two authors (whom logic forces to admit that, if things are so bad at court, they have remained at court themselves because they are foolish, weak, ambitious, and habit-bound) is the same.

Guevara's idea of combining both the dispraise of court life and a commendation of a life of retirement in the same work seems to be his original contribution to the development of the anticourtier theme. After the publication of the *Menosprecio de corte y alabanza de aldea*, it became the most important European embodiment of the theme in modern literature. He was able, with remarkable sensitivity, to absorb and then express contemporary anxieties, presenting them in terms or images which are found both in medieval works like Gregory's *Moralia in Job* and in "modern," heavily classicized works like Aeneas Silvius's *De Miseriis Curialium*. That these anxieties (such as the tensions created by the aristocrat's desire to stay at court in order to increase his wealth and his fear of punishment for greed or envy) are very old ones does not make them less poignant; that the forms of expression can be traced back to Hesiod does not make them less modern.[6]

III *Criticism*

The contents of the *Dispraise* are a development of ideas already discussed at some length by Guevara in chapter XVI of the *Favored Courtier*, "where the author warns favorites of princes to beware of the deceits of the world and not to allow themselves to grow old at court if they wish to die a Christian death" (*F.C.*, p. 199). Guevara says that he has scolded friends who, he thinks, need to return to their homes and give up court life; but, like the "demented" acquaintance who had lived so long at court that he "had callouses on his conscience" (*F.C.*, p. 206), not a single one has ever taken his advice. "It would be sound advice for those who have grown old—not only old, but rancid—at the courts of princes for them, in the days that they have left, to pride themselves on living like Christians instead of acting like courtiers, so that if they have given their flour to the world, they may at least give the bran to God" (*F.C.*, p. 206). Not only the thought but even the wording of the latter part of this chapter is found echoed in many places in the *Dispraise* (compare, e.g., p. 9 of *Dispraise*).

The *Favored Courtier* is addressed to the favorites of princes and to courtiers, the *Dispraise* is dedicated to a king; but in fact it treats of the disadvantages of life at court for the ordinary gentleman and the benefits of voluntary retirement from court— neither of which subjects could be of very great interest to a king, one would suppose. Occasionally, Guevara even slips into the type of direct address to the courtier which he had employed in the *Favored Courtier*: "Believe me, sir courtier...." (114); "Let the courtier who hears or reads this ..." (115). In this work, Guevara poses as the old courtier who looks back on his years at court and who ruefully confesses his own ambition and vanity. He gives the reader a thumbnail sketch of his life in the first few pages of the book, and in the final three chapters, he makes a public confession (185) of his sins. This biographical element gives unity to the work, which would otherwise be merely variations on a theme already treated in more interesting detail in the *Favored Courtier*.

Fray Antonio has organized the subject into chapters (I–III) on problems of choosing a way of life that will allow one to develop his virtues and avoid temptation, and on the dangers of giving advice in so serious a matter. But the "virtuous, gentle, honest, and quiet" (53) courtier should undoubtedly withdraw from court.[7] Chapters IV–VII contrast the discomforts of court life with the healthful life of the villager. Chapters V–VII, using a mock-legal formula, catalog the "rights" of small-town existence: "It is a privilege of the village that everyone may go about not only unaccompanied [by servants] and in shirt-sleeves, but that he may also travel or take a walk without owning a mule or maintaining a horse" (75).[8] Chapters VIII–XV describe the laxity, hypocrisy, and anxieties of life at court. These chapters (IV–XV) are almost entirely free of erudition and classical references.

In chapters XVI–XVII, Guevara shows how well-disciplined were the courts and cities of antiquity,[9] and he collects a number of cases of famous men of antiquity who retired from court at the peak of their careers. The contrast between the retirement of, say, Pericles and his own refusal to leave court provides a logical transition back to the personal revelations of the author.

There are, in my opinion, three portions of the book which deserve extra attention. These are chapter IV, "On the life which the courtier should lead after he has left the court," passages which deal with "delinquent" types (especially chapter XI), and the final confession.

Bishop Guevara was a natural psychologist, and he realized fully the emotional problems created by moving from the troublesome but exciting life of the capital to the often boring life of some provincial town, where petty annoyances become magnified. He does not conceal the difficulties, and he does not paint the village as a paradise full of guileless rustics. "After the courtier has come home to rest, he must take care that he does not let it become irksome to him; otherwise if he was bored in the palace, he will be desperate in the village. The solitude ... the importunity of his wife, the mischief of his children, the carelessness of the servants, and even the gossip of his neighbors are bound to annoy and depress him occasionally, but when he remembers that he has escaped from the court and from its dangerous gulf, he will consider it well worth it" (61–62). "He must also avoid vicious, lazy, mendacious, and malicious men, of which small towns are full; for if the courts of princes are full of envy, so in villages there is much malice" (63).

The antidote for boredom is a program of charitable and religious activities. Guevara observes in both the *Favored Courtier* and *Dispraise* that it is possible to be virtuous anywhere, even at court, but he seems to think that the ordinary gentleman —not the influential courtier or the great nobles—will have the means and the prestige in his small hometown to do good, whereas at court he is restricted by his income and by his relative unimportance. If the courtier's (that is, the gentleman's) real goal is a Christian death, then he may more easily prepare himself away from the temptations and ambitions of court life.

Skipping from Guevara's plans for the retired gentleman to

the last chapters, one can see more evidence of his profound knowledge of human nature. No doubt his experience as a preacher had taught him that man is insatiably curious about the activities of his fellows and that there is no more successful attention-getter for a sermon than a personal anecdote. Guevara used this device in all of his works, but nowhere more successfully than in the *Dispraise*. The prologue and other passages present the author as a man who has "known the court from very early childhood" (176), held various posts, and seen his fortunes rise and fall. But these exterior facts are not nearly so interesting as the confession of his weaknesses, failures, and unworthy motives, particularly since the penitent is a famous author, a bishop, an official historian, a member of the highest government advisory board, an aristocrat. The confession, furthermore, gives the impression of complete sincerity in spite of the orchestrated cadences and rhymes of its prose.

Perhaps Américo Castro was correct when he said that it was the self-flagellation which was novel and appealing to contemporary readers, though it could hardly have seemed too novel to readers brought up on St. Augustine. Nevertheless, in the days before the flowering of the picaresque novel, such personal revelations are rare in Spanish prose. One wonders if they are not but another example of his preacher's stock-in-trade?

Perhaps the most interesting section of the *Dispraise* from a literary historian's vantage point is that which deals with what one might call "proto-picaresque" types. One of Guevara's arguments for leaving court is that it is full of wicked men: "I do not deny that at the courts of princes many find salvation, nor do I deny that away from them many find damnation; but I am convinced that since vices are so accessible there, extremely vicious men are at home there" (124). Guevara distinguishes ten types of "vice-ridden" idlers and delinquents who flourish in the lax moral atmosphere of the capital. There is the well-born young man who enters the service of his family's hereditary rivals or social inferiors, not because he wishes to be a peacemaker between factions but because he is greedy for the fancy livery or meals or horse which they offer. And there is the young gentleman who earns his meals as a professional gossip, roaming the streets all day in search of scandalous tidbits and news. These two classes may be shameful, but they are not dishonest. A worse type of men are the swindlers who attach themselves to some unwary newcomer, promising to introduce him to the right people, show him how to expedite his business, and take him to the red-light district, and who steal the greenhorn's clothing and mule and help him "lighten his purse" (120). Equally bad are the "vagabonds" who pretend to be gentlemen fallen on hard times (though they can afford to maintain "a page, two servant-boys, a horse, a mule, and even a mistress" [121]), and who depend on the charity of wealthy lords who believe their tales. One rung lower are the confidence men who have already been exposed at court and who therefore work on gullible clerics, getting free meals at monasteries or persuading confessors to ask their well-to-do protégés for a "restitution." These evil types eat the food destined for the honest poor. Even lower are the rogues who hang about the market place in order to assist butlers and cooks who come to buy and from whom they beg or filch food.

Then there are the genuine criminals. "There is another kind of rake at court who by fours or threes go about together in gangs and bands; and their system of supporting themselves is to scatter and go through the palaces, inns, stores, and even churches during the day; and if someone (for his sins) is careless with his cape or cap or sword or indeed of the purse that he carries in his pocket, in the twinkling of an eye—he will never find what he lost or meet the man who took it" (122). Pimps, dishonest gamblers, and madams (in whose houses "there is a better selection of girls than there is of eels in the fishmarket" [123]) complete the picture.

Undoubtedly Guevara is drawing a perfectly realistic gallery of characters from the sixteenth-century underworld which could be substantiated with documentary proof. José Deleito y Piñuela's *La mala vida en la España de Felipe IV* (Immoral Life in the Spain of Philip IV [Madrid: Espasa-Calpe, 1948]), though it deals with mid-seventeenth-century Spain, contains numerous parallels, both authentic and literary. But Guevara is interested in the misguided types he describes as symbols of general decadence, not in their own right, and to them he opposes the virtuous gentleman who retreats from the capital in pursuit of spiritual perfection. Such spiritual types are also quite "realistic" for the Spain of the sixteenth century and are as interesting to the student of history as the delinquents.

But in Spanish literature, the con-man, not the upright squire, becomes the subject of a genre, and it would be hard to find in pre-*Lazarillo* popular literature a passage more suggestive of the literary possibilities of "picaresque" types than these pages in the *Dispraise*. The poor courtier struggling to preserve a seedy dignity is well sketched by Guevara in the *Favored Courtier*; in the *Dispraise*, scoundrels who gull recently arrived provincials are brought to life in sharp, witty descriptions; it seems but a step from these free-floating elements to their logical arrangement in the simple frame-story of *Lazarillo*, though one recognizes that such "simple" steps are the work of genius. If Guevara did not contribute directly—as he may well have done—to the composition of *Lazarillo*, he undoubtedly strengthened the literary currents which made it possible, and almost all of Guevara's scoundrels could be illustrated by passages from later picaresque novels.

CHAPTER 7

The Art of Navigation

I Contents

G UEVARA composed the *Art of Navigation* (*Arte de marear*)
after his *Favored Courtier* and addressed it, like the
Favored Courtier, to Francisco de los Cobos. In a dedicatory
letter, dated from Valladolid, 25 June 1539, Guevara describes
the work as intended for a *pasatiempo,* for shipboard reading.

Guevara begins by reviewing the preposterous things which
historians have written on the origins of sea travel, "so that those
who read may know that we have also read it [ancient history]
and believed very little of it" (11–12).[1] He rejects, for example,
the accounts of the galley of Terison the Syracusan, which had
two prows and two sterns, thirty rooms below deck, and a fish
tank that held twenty thousand gallons of water; and of the
galley of Lucullus which was so large that it accommodated a
bullfight ("and what is more, the sailors made a fortune selling
places for people to watch the bull fights"). He asserts that the
real inventor of the galley was Theseus, the killer of the *mino-
centauro,* though St. Isidore attributes primitive efforts at making
small craft to the Lydians. All historians, however, agree that
a Greek perfected shipbuilding before the battle of Marathon.
The bishop aptly cites a number of famous philosophers who
have spoken against sea travel. "What is sane about a man who
lives on a ship? What more appropriate song can you sing on
board ship than that response for the dead which goes *Memento
mei Deus, quia ventus est vita mea*? What is your life but wind,
since on a galley the principal occupation is talking about wind,
watching the wind, hoping for the wind, waiting for the wind,
running from the wind, or sailing with the wind?" (19–20). As
the Roman consul Fabius Torquatus said so eloquently, it is
104

risky to fight with men, but it is madness to battle the winds. "Therefore the words of my theme are true: *La vida de la galera, déla Dios a quien la quiera*" (21).

"Sea travel is relatively safe when [your ship] follows the coastline, but when it puts out to sea, it is very dangerous; from which one may gather that galleys were invented for robbing rather than for sailing" (22). Guevara supports this thesis with numerous examples of the evil uses to which galleys have been put, such as the exploits of notable pirates of ancient times: "Cleonidas was a pirate in the time of King Ptolemy, and he roamed the seas as a corsair for twenty-two years, during seven of which it is written that no man ever saw him leave his galley or set foot on land. This Cleonidas was lame and cross-eyed, and not in vain did Nature set her mark on him, because he was extremely cruel to those he captured, and he was false to those with whom he had dealings. One of the tortures to which this accursed corsair subjected the enemies who fell into his hands was to tie their hands and feet and give them an enema of boiling oil" (24). Which he did, he said, to burn the innards which harbored ill feelings toward him. Having dealt with the evil origins and progress of seafaring, Bishop Guevara turns to the hardships of shipboard life, or as he sarcastically calls them, "the splendid conditions of the ship and great delights with which it is endowed" (26). Aside from the perpetual fear of pirates or shipwreck, there is the complete loss of social status and an enforced familiarity—which the bishop obviously finds distasteful. Among the other "joys" of the life at sea are the absence of "the conversation of ladies, delicate food, fragrant wines, comforting odors, cold water, and other such delicacies" (27). On the contrary, the biscuit is often rotten, the water so foul that "the captain gives very fastidious [passengers] permission to hold their noses when they drink it" (27–28), the wine frequently sour, and the meat "disgusting to see, hard as the devil to chew, as salty as raging thirst to eat, [and] as indigestible as rocks" (28).

If the food is bad, the conditions under which the passengers eat it are worse: the few dishes, little or no clean linen, small space, and scarcity of water for washing reduce them to wiping their hands on their shirts or their beards and to eating on the

floor "like Moors" or on their laps "like women." Fray Antonio
alludes in passing to other conditions which modern travelers
would find appalling. There are, of course, no private accommodations of any kind. Each passenger exercises, sits, and sleeps
where he can. Those who want a special place to sit or sleep
have to bribe the captain or boatswain. Bathing and washing are
impossible. Passengers spend the night in their clothes. Seasick
passengers are sources of amusement to the more experienced,
etc., etc. There is no privacy for personal hygiene, and the filth,
fleas, lice, mice, and occasionally cats and dogs become well-
nigh intolerable in such close quarters. Guevara describes the
problems created by the numerous storms: with the violent
movement, it is dangerous to make a fire and impossible to
serve food; passengers must crowd below deck to make room
for the activities of the crew, and "the confusion, shouting, and
noise of the sailors is more frightening than the fury and fierce-
ness of the sea" (31). In storms, such temporary shelters as the
tents stretched over the decks are removed, leaving the passengers to the mercy of sun and rain.

Guevara is somewhat heavier-handed in his descriptions of the
criminal immorality of sailors. The crew use their position to
steal with impunity from the passengers, or to extort from them
what we would call tips. Gambling and cheating are common;
fugitives are protected from the law by the crews, which are
often made up of criminals. The sailors are in effect exempt from
the usual religious obligations: the bishop says that when he
asked the sailors to see their *cédulas* (certificates which showed
when they had last been to confession), they showed him a
deck of cards.

The behavior aboard ship passes the bounds of immorality
and becomes criminal when the crew lands to take on firewood
or water; they desolate the countryside worse than an invading
enemy, stealing, cutting down trees, raping, and kidnapping:
"frost, hail, and locust do not do so much damage in a hard year
as the crew do in only half a day" (38).

For the passengers the final indignity comes when disembarking. By custom they leave behind their equipment and un-
used supplies, and yet they must tip the entire crew and make
a show of gratitude and friendship.

The ships were, to modern taste, appallingly flimsy, small, and ill-equipped. Anyone who has boarded the replicas of Columbus's ships in the harbor of Barcelona has nothing but awe for the suicidal bravery of the crew that set out in them. These tiny ships make Guevara's remarks about the discomforts of life aboard ship much more understandable.

Guevara next provides for the inexperienced traveler a glossary of sailor's jargon, which is as extraordinary, he says, as their way of life. The tone of this chapter of useful phrases is one of tolerant amusement at the sailors' stubborn refusal to use the obvious word.

Finally, fray Antonio gives some practical advice on preparations for a voyage. First, of course, the traveler must prepare to meet death in a Christian fashion; he should purge his soul of sins and his body of unhealthy humors. Then he should book passage on a new ship with an experienced crew and a reputation for good luck because "it does not seem to me to be sound advice for anyone to risk his life where he knows that some one else has lost his life and his honor" (49). The passenger should also cultivate the good will of the officers and crew in advance and upon boarding, in order to insure himself of as much comfort as possible. He should pack only warm, sturdy clothing, a small bedroll, preserved meats, fruits, wine, and modest tableware, all of which he should show to the officers on boarding and have registered by the purser, to avoid theft. He should provide himself with entertaining reading material as well as a book of hours, "because of the three pastimes that there are on the sea, to wit, gambling, gossiping, and reading, the most profitable and least harmful is reading" (52). It might also be sensible to take fishing tackle for calm days, "because it is better for his soul and indeed for his purse to be fishing from the bow than to be gambling in the stern" (52). Dried fruits and preserves are healthful and may be eaten when one is seasick or when bad weather prevents cooking; plain honest food like garlic, onions, vinegar, and oil do not make one seasick and are less likely to be stolen. He should take perfume and smelling salts, because the stench of bilge becomes so offensive that it causes fainting or nausea unless one has something to smell. And to prevent sea-sickness and dizziness, a small packet of saffron placed over the heart works admirably. "I followed this advice myself, and it preserved my life" (54).

II *Sources*

Thanks to the excellent new edition of R. O. Jones, the sources of this work are known, and I can do no better than quote Jones's introduction: "In this book Guevara draws on Pliny, Plutarch (in Latin), Athenaeus, Seneca, Justinus, Publilius Syrus and Isidore; in addition he refers (without, as far as I can tell, using them) to Diogenes Laertius and Hermogenes. Some of these authors he probably knew not in the original but in digests. . . . For this study I have traced most of Guevara's sources, but almost certainly not all. To attempt to go further would probably be pointless, since the fruits of further investigation would be disproportionately small in relation to the effort expended. To search out Guevara's main sources has its value, however, and is not merely a sop to a scholar's unhealthy appetite for pedantry; it allows one to define and evaluate the nature of Guevara's achievement as a creative writer. For the main interest in such investigation is not just to establish that Guevara borrowed, but what he made of his borrowings" (x–xii). Jones has found that Guevara uses material from a poor text of Pliny, *Naturalis Historia VII;* a Latin edition of Plutarch's *Lives* and *Apophthegmata;* Athenaeus's *Deipnosoph-istae,* in an unknown Latin translation, apparently; Seneca's "Ad Helviam matrem de consolatione;" Justinus's *Epitoma Historiarum Philippicarum Pompei Trogi;* Publilius Syrus's *Cato;* and Isidore's *Etymologiae.*

Professor Jones shows with illuminating examples how Guevara takes small passages from his texts and converts them into anecdotes or colorful details which scarcely resemble the original source. He explains the bishop's puzzling elaborations as an obsession with words, a manifestation of literary ambition which could be satisfied by writing books for "men-about-court" of limited education, whose half-hearted interest in prestigious antiquity was satisfied by Guevara's mixture of real names and fictitious action.

III *Form and Style*

The form into which Guevara casts his little book is that of a sermon. Sermon parodies are not rare (R. O. Jones, p. xii, reminds us of Diego de San Pedro's *Sermón* on love), but Guevara's has the added charm of being a mock sermon by a real preacher.

Guevara begins his sermon with the following titles: "Here begins the *Book of the Inventors of the Art of Seamanship and the Hardships of Sea Travel*, compiled by the illustrious lord don Antonio de Guevara, Bishop of Mondoñedo, Preacher, Chronicler, Councilor of H. M., Which Takes the Form of a Sermon. Here Follow the Theme and Introduction" (7).

The "scripture" on which the sermon is based is a rhyming proverb, "Let God give shipboard life to whoever will have it." The introduction touches on the value of experience and of proverbs, the quintessence of experience: "The theme of our sermon, which says, 'Let God give [. . . etc.]' was, we can be sure, not invented by the philosophers of Athens but by sailors on the sea, for which reason we can with reason believe it and esteem it, for they invented it on the basis of experience, not things guessed at or dreamed" (8). Guevara states his three divisions: "In this sermon we shall speak of the origin of shipbuilding, the language spoken on shipboard, and what one needs to provide himself with for sea travel, all of which things, when they have been stated and explained, will, I am sure, astound many—and amuse a few. . . . Let this suffice for an introduction, and since time is short and the matter long, it only remains for me to beg you to be attentive to what I shall preach to you and to watch out for what applies to you. And if someone begins to doze, let his companion gouge him in the ribs and wake him up, because he who does not profit by our doctrine will take ship in an evil hour" (8). After three chapters (on the history, invention, and dangers of navigation), Guevara repeats the theme: as the consul Fabius Torquatus once said, "Fighting with men is a matter of luck, but fighting with the winds is madness. Thus the words of my theme are true, 'Let God give life on shipboard,' etc." And he repeats it after the chapters on pirates, the hardships of sailing, the "gibberish" spoken by sailors, and the properties of the sea.

The concluding portion of the book, on what the traveler should take with him, ends thus: "I followed all of this advice myself on the voyage which we made with my lord and master Caesar when he went to conquer great Tunisia in Africa, and it saved my life—I mean the life of the body, for the life of the spirit will be given to us in heaven, *ad quam nos perducat Jesus Christus* ... [etc.] *Amen.*" This is the traditional conclusion of all sermons, which still survives in such prayers as "Now unto God the Father ...," etc. Chapters V-VII are a list of the "privileges" of life aboard ship. R. O. Jones (xii) observes that these chapters "read like amusing parodies of *fueros* or similar documents."

IV *Contemporary Allusions*

I know of no other work in Spanish which gives so graphic a picture of life aboard ship. The anonymous novel *Estebanillo González* supplements and verifies what Guevara says, from the point of view of the semicriminal crew, for apparently conditions of sea travel had changed little by the 1630s, when the picaresque autobiography was written. One finds innumerable references to sea travel in early Spanish literature, naturally, but other authors merely took for granted its hardships—which had after all existed since ancient times and were to exist until the nineteenth century—and felt no need to describe what everyone already knew. Guevara's pose as a much-put-upon passenger writing to a friend makes it logical to review all these discomforts and to comment on them. Parts of the book, for example, the last chapter, bring home to the modern reader, who will naturally delight in the quaintness of the advice as well as the aptness of a great deal of it, how little suggestions for the inexperienced traveler have changed in four hundred years. Advice on what to wear, shipboard etiquette, tipping the crew, how to avoid sea-sickness and so on still form the core of travel advice in the brochures of shipping companies and travel books. Sea travel, for all the modern amenities, still maintains many of the traditional elements which Guevara describes, such as the absolute social superiority of the captain and crew, the temporary familiarities, and the obsession with food, drink, and pastimes like gambling. Humans still apparently react in identical fashion to boredom and cramped conditions, and Guevara's witty description is accurate, original, and must have amused greatly the royal secretary who had had so much experience of the sea.

There are two serious concerns lightly touched on in passing— concerns which appear frequently in Guevara's writings, the problems of piracy and the depredations of armies. The danger and incalculable economic damage inflicted by pirates is so remote from us that we cannot imagine the indignation which even the mention of piracy must have aroused in Guevara's readers. Guevara plays on this when he lists piracy as one of the dire consequences of the invention of sailing: "Before Theseus the Greek invented shipbuilding, one does not read that there were corsairs or pirates on the sea; but after galleys began to be built, there has always been someone to sack on land and rob on the sea . . . since a galley is so troublesome and so costly, I do not believe that anyone would spend his own money on it unless he planned to pay for it with someone else's property" (22). The plain inference is that there is a thin line between government policy (shipbuilding for defense) and criminality (privateering as a business venture which benefits the government). Such disapproval is consistent with his condemnation of all military activity not absolutely necessary for defense, of all commercial activity not necessary for survival, and with his favorite idea of the relativity of evil. Under some conditions, antisocial behavior may be criminal, while the same behavior in socially sanctioned form may be patriotic.

The bishop in several places describes the suffering of country people at the hands of "friendly" armies and navies which devastated the land and from whom there was no protection, since their activities were "legal." This is another point on which *Estabanillo González* confirms Guevara's observations. In the *Art of Navigation*, Guevara cynically includes the immunity from punishment for sacking the coastal towns as one of the privileges of sailors: "It is a privilege of the galleys that when the soldiers, oarsmen, boatmen, and even the passengers go ashore near some good, prosperous town there is no grove they do not cut down, no beehive that they do not rob, tree they do not pull down, dovecote they do not investigate, game they do not hunt, garden they do not desolate, girl they do not tumble, woman they do not seduce, boy they do not kidnap, slave they do not carry off, vineyard they do not harvest, bacon they do not seize, or clothing they do not steal; so that in a bad year, frost and hail and locusts do not do as much damage as those on a galley do in half a day" (38) To quote Professor Jones once more: "*El arte de marear* is one of Guevara's most attractive works. It has the human interest of a document drawn from real life. In all he wrote, Guevara's personality shines through, and nowhere more clearly than here.... If any of Guevara's works can be expected to appeal to modern readers, this is the one" (xi–xiii).

CHAPTER 8

The Familiar Letters

I *Contents*

THE variety of subject matter in Guevara's *Familiar Letters* (*Epístolas familiares*)—one of the principal charms of the collection—makes it difficult to summarize this work. Perhaps the simplest way to present the contents is to group the letters into large categories and select examples from each. Guevara's own arrangement has no chronological or thematic basis, so that a regrouping of the letters does not diminish their artistry. Another problem in reducing the *Familiar Letters* to manageable units about which one can make general statements is that many of them are neither letters nor familiar. They are what we would classify as essays, a very ancient form brought to perfection by Plutarch and other Greco-Roman writers, and imitated by Guevara, Pedro Mexía, and innumerable sixteenth-century writers, including Montaigne. The one-line salutation and formal close do not change their essential nature.

The following large groupings provide a fair sampling of the collection: (1) sermons; (2) erudite letters, on historical, archaeological, and medical subjects, including "translations" of ancient letters; (3) moral letters, on the correction of vices, on rulership, friendship, marriage, etc.; (4) letters and a speech on the rebellion of the communes; and (5) familiar letters. Virtually every letter contains classical embellishments, and there are a number which would fall reasonably into more than one of the divisions.

The Prologue of the letters is the shortest of all Guevara's forewords, perhaps because it is not dedicated to anyone. In it, the bishop complains that various persons have appropriated his letters and published them under their own names, a misfortune suffered by Plato, Phalaris, Seneca, and Cicero—the

113

greatest letter writers of antiquity. "Seeing therefore that some were stealing them from me, others were printing them, others were publishing them as their own work, I decided to revise them and to communicate them to everyone, because the educated, discreet reader will recognize by their style those that have been stolen from me. So, by reviewing my memoranda and hunting up my rough copies, I have found these few letters that follow, many of which are printed just as they were written; others have been corrected and polished, because one often writes to friends things that must not be revealed to everyone."[1]

Sermons make up more than a quarter of the collection, and we shall take them as our first category (from vol. I, epistles nos. 1, 2, 8, 15, 16, 19, 31, 33, 37, 59; from vol. II, nos. 1, 2, 4–12, 15, 16, 20, 23, 25, 28, 29, 37, 39, 43).[2]

Guevara was aware that matter prepared for oral delivery was rarely so effective when merely read. It is already hard for modern readers to evaluate Guevara's eloquence, since both the matter and the style of delivery are now considered quaint relics of an overly religious century; his remarks on the pallor of written sermons are therefore doubly interesting: "What you ask of me, sir—that I send you, just as I delivered it, that sermon which I preached before his Majesty—is something that I never do or should do, because though it is in my power to send you what I say, I cannot send you the skill with which I preach it, because that pomp and energy which God gives to my tongue at the time, He rarely gives to my pen afterward. . . . The difference between the plan and the house, the model and the building, the figure and the drawing, the natural and the painted, *that* is the difference between hearing a sermon in the pulpit and reading it in print, because only the eyes are satisfied with the writing, but the heart soars with the spoken word" (vol. I, pp. 59, 60). "The preacher who writes down what he said in the pulpit puts himself in danger of losing his reputation, because the spirit which a great preacher gives to what he says is more important than all he says to us" (I, 125).

The sermons show imagination and variety that can scarcely be epitomized in a few paragraphs, but some of the more significant are described below. Number 19 from volume I provides an example of Guevara's use of "suspense" in sermons.

The bishop purports to find a contradiction in the scriptural text (Ps. 55.15 "Let them go down quick into hell"), which he later manages to resolve. This is an old technique, out of favor now since Padre Isla's day, but one which must have had an added piquancy in the days when a Nebrija or an Erasmus could run afoul of the Inquisition for finding errors in the Scriptures. The solution to the puzzle in this sermon—one cannot go to hell while still alive ("quick")—is that the psalmist wants men to visualize hell in order to see the horrible consequences of sin. This is very sound psychology, in the bishop's opinion: "Let him who will, make a pilgrimage to Montserrat, let him go to Santiago for the jubilee, let him make vows to Our Lady of Guadalupe, let him go to St. Lazarus of Seville, let him send alms to the Holy House, let him have novenas to the Crucifix of Burgos and offer his goods to St. Anthony of Castro; but I want no other pilgrimage but the pilgrimage to hell.... It seems to me that he who has a picture of hell in his chapel has a rather good devotional painting, because many more people abstain from sinning out of fear of punishment than out of love of heaven" (127–28).

Only ten of the sixty-nine letters of volume I are sermons or *précis* of sermons, but volume II has twenty-two sermons out of forty-three letters. Particularly interesting are the fully developed sermons, numbers 1, 2, 11, 12, 16, most of the others being too brief to be anything but sketches. Numbers 23, 28, and 29 are sketchy accounts of public debates with Jews held in Naples and Rome. The theology is dull, but occasional touches of unexpected humor and goodwill temper the anti-Semitism typical of the age. Guevara reminds his Neapolitan addressee, a certain Baruch Japheo, that their discussions were so heated that they seemed like duels rather than debates, and that the "seconds" prevented them from pummeling each other. Guevara was piqued by Japheo's smug insistence that no Christian could interpret a certain biblical verse, and to add interest to the encounter, the bishop and the Jew wagered a Jewish pastry and a pint of wine: "so that in the wager, one showed himself to be a drunkard and the other a glutton" (279). Guevara concludes the letter by saying that he is continuing his debates with the Jews in Rome every Saturday, "and to tell you the truth, I am having as little luck making Christians out of them as they are in making a Jew out of me. God keep you; and may it please Him to bring you to the holy Catholic faith" (285).

The next category, the erudite letters, contains those on classical and historical subjects, fictitious letters from antiquity, and the like (I, 3, 4, 23–25, 27, 28, 30, 32, 40, 44, 45, 54, 56, 63–65; II, 17, 19, 26, 30–34, 40). Most of them are answers to questions put to the bishop by important correspondents.

Number 3, volume I, is a letter to the emperor, who has asked the famous preacher to identify some specimens from the imperial coin collection. Guevara selects five specimens to elucidate. They are imaginary, apparently, but Guevara makes them "texts" for a little discourse on law. He is, as usual, more interested in the moral values of the relics than in their history. (The great sixteenth-century Spanish classicist and numismatist Antonio Agustín, archbishop of Tarragona, singled out this letter for his scorn.) The next epistle is the text of a speech delivered before the court of Germaine de Foix, widow of Ferdinand the Catholic. It begins with the usual familiarities and a note of relaxed humor that recalls the soirées of *The Courtier*: "And since your majesty is pleased to permit your ladies-in-waiting and their suitors to be present at this talk, kindly order them not to make faces at each other or gesture, for they have sworn that they will distract me or cut me short" (28). The subject is Lycurgus, philosopher-king (according to Guevara) of the Lacedemonians. Guevara describes Lycurgus and recounts his life briefly, then gives a sampling of the laws which he enacted: equal division of all property; prohibition of banquets, superfluous clothing, baths ("they weaken the strength of the members" [33]) and perfumes ("inciters to vice" [33]); respect for elders; outlawing of elaborate tombs, of gamblers and actors, money, sailing, dowries, etc., etc. One can imagine how such laws would catch the fancy of the well-fed, well-dressed, pleasure-loving courtiers whom Guevara is amusing.

Guevara deciphers an ancient inscription for a friend, who got it in Rome (no. 27). It is the oracle of a sybil named Délphica, originally given to King Romulus on a piece of bark, later explained by another sybil named Erithea. This fiction, of a type which Guevara seemed to enjoy, is a fashionably "classical" version of the guessing games and puzzles that were considered good parlor entertainment.

Number 54 is a history of medicine, which discusses its benefits and dangers and the author's opinion of medical service. Aside from the usual mixture of classical erudition and fiction, there are curious observations on contemporary practice and theory, as well as Guevara's outspoken criticisms of doctors he has dealt with: "In Alcalá, I also spoke with Dr. Cartagena, and he prescribed [for my gout] a plaster of ox dung, mouse droppings, oat-meal, nettle leaves, roses, and fried scorpions, to be applied to my thigh, and the benefit which I received from it was that it kept me from sleeping for three nights—and I paid the apothecary who made it six *reales!*" (343). This letter is one of the longest, with twenty pages of printed text in the modern edition.

Number 64 is addressed to the viceroy of Cataluña, the archbishop of Zaragoza, who had asked Guevara for one of Marcus Aurelius's unpublished love letters: "A thousand times I have regretted having translated those love letters, but the count of Nassau, the Prince of Orange, and my cousin Don Pedro [Vélez] de Guevara... made me do what I did not want to do, nor should do. Being, as I was, of illustrious blood, a theologian by profession, a monk by persuasion, and a courtier by condition, the office of lover was quite inappropriate for me..." (451). However, to comply with the archbishop's request, Guevara claims to have searched until he found the letter which he publishes with the following ironical protestations: "On my faith as a Christian I promise you, and on my word as a gentleman I swear to you, that the letter is translated *ad pedem litterae* and faithfully copied" (452). The letter is from Marcus Aurelius to Popilión, captain of the Parthians, on the vagaries of Fortune, stoicism, and clemency to enemies.

Category 3, the moral, includes I, 11, 18, 20–22, 29, 34, 35, 50, 55; and II, 24, 35, 41, 42. Number 11 is to the Marquis of Pescara (the friar's first cousin, once removed), grandson of Juan de Guevara, Grand Seneschal of the Kingdom of Naples. Pescara is besieging Marseilles, and Guevara cannot but remind him that war between Christian rulers is unjustifiable: "... we see nothing but wars among Christians, while the Moors are allowed to prosper and live in peace. It is such a difficult matter for me that, though I can discuss it, I cannot understand it; for we daily see that God, in his secret judgments, permits churches where His name is praised to be destroyed and razed, while mosques where they insult Him remain untouched and free" (81). The body of the letter lays before the marquis the duties of the good soldier, for example, "avoid unjust damage, correct blasphemers, protect the innocent, punish the impudent, pay the army, prevent plundering, and keep your word to the enemy" (82).

Number 22 treats of the vices which arise out of unlimited freedom. The Italian states are sad examples of this unfortunate condition, and Rome is the worst: "Oh what distance there is between Italian customs and pure Christian law, because the one says do whatever you want, the other, do what you ought. . . . The one, that you should believe in Christ alone, the other, that you should try to get rich" (143–44). Number 34 is to an elderly gentleman who has asked the Franciscan for a love letter to send to his mistress; Guevara, scandalized by the request, replies in a withering letter: "At your age, one does not wear perforated silk shoes, Toledan cap, knee-length coat, embroidered gaiters, pearl gorget at the throat, a gold medallion on the cap, and a livery of his lady-friend's colors . . ." (221). In the following letter, he details the proper activity for a man of sixty-three: "Old gentlemen of your age must be so correct in what they say and so exemplary in what they do that not only will they not be seen doing anything wicked but not even saying improper words, for one willful and dissolute old man will suffice to ruin an entire nation" (226).

Number 55, one of the longest in the collection (27 pages) is a letter to a newly wed pair of teenagers, which begins with such appallingly tactless remarks as "you have a long time to enjoy the matrimony and indeed to mourn the marriage" or "it saddens me to see you married at such a tender age" (363–64). Guevara pursues the subject relentlessly: "When people marry very young, very great harm ensues for them: [the women] are crippled in childbirth, their strength fails, [the couple] are burdened with children, they spend their inheritance, they are jealous of each other, they do not know the meaning of honor, they do not understand how to run a household, their love for each other dies, and they assume new cares, so that from having married so young, they later come to live discontented or live apart when they grow old" (365). Perhaps the truth of all this is undisputable, particularly in an age of large families, high infant-mortality rates, and deaths from parturition, but the letter is scarcely what one writes to newlyweds; obviously Guevara only intended it as a "model" for correspondence on the subject of marriage. From the evils of early marriage, the celibate author moves on to the flaws of women (the hauteur of noble ladies, the dangers of a beautiful wife, the want of housewifely skills in an educated woman, etc. [366]). Thence, he begins a list of precepts for successful marriage: "The rules which I wish to give here to those who are about to be married—and even to those who are already married—may not help them to live more content, but at least they will help them avoid many annoyances" (367).

Number 35 is to "a secret friend." This letter, written from Valencian territory during the time that Guevara, as commissioner, was preaching and baptizing converted Moriscos, attempts to persuade a Valencian gentleman that the custom of addressing converts to Christianity as "Moor, dog, Jew, swine," or "infidel" (378–79) is "neither chivalrous, nor Christian, nor even courtly" (377). "Are you perchance God, of whom the prophet says *scrutans corda et renes*, that you should know whether Cidi Abducarim is a renegade Moor or apostate Christian? Have you perchance measured your merits against his and put your faith in the balance with his? ... *Qui dixerit fratri suo racha, reus erit Gehennae*, said Christ in the Gospel. ... I ask you now, which is a greater insult, to call one a fool or to call him a Moorish dog or dirty Jew? As for me, I dare say that I would prefer to be called a fool, and an idiot, and even an imbecile, rather than be called a bad Christian, because being called a fool affects [only] my honor but being called a heretic touches my soul *and* defames my good name" (379). That it is commonplace to "call the newly converted *Moor* or *swine* at every other word" is no excuse at all. The unconverted can see no benefit in becoming Christians when Christians continue to look down upon them and call them opprobrious names.

Guevara's genuine interest in his converts and his compassion for their difficult situation should not be taken as an example of *social* tolerance, however. Guevara was too conditioned to the lines of class, blood, and wealth to understand even the modest social equality sought by some of the more radical *comuneros*. His Valencian friend infringes Christian laws when he presumes to judge a man's spiritual worth in God's eyes; if he had called the convert a stupid peasant or villein (a term of derision often used in the comedy of the seventeenth century), Guevara would not have raised an eyebrow.

The fourth category is composed of the letters which touch upon the rebellion of the communes, including I, 7, 47–49, 51, 52, 62; and II, 18. Letters 47 to 49 are addressed to the irascible old bishop of Zamora, who was eventually hanged for his part in the comunero upheaval. Fray Antonio claims, during one of his diplomatic missions, to have persuaded Pedro Girón, the most prestigious noble on the side of the rebels, to defect to the imperial side before the battle of Tordesillas. It would be risky to deny that the bishop of Zamora actually wrote a letter to Guevara out of sheer frustration and rage over the defection of Girón, but it seems unlikely that a harried leader of the rebels would take time to write to the friar merely to vent his spleen. This is, however, what Guevara would have us believe. In response to the attack, Guevara heaps scorn on the motives of the bishop and his fellow "traitors" and belittles their efforts with several amusing anecdotes: he affirms that he has heard of a half-mad Basque priest who, when he announced celebrations for the week, asked his parishioners to pray for His Majesty, King Juan de Padilla, and Queen María de Padilla. "These prayers lasted about three weeks, after which Juan de Padilla passed through with his army, and since the soldiers who were billeted in the priest's house carried off his mistress, drank up his wine, killed his chickens, and ate his bacon, he said in church on the following Sunday, '. . . from now on, do not pray for him but for the King Charles . . . and to hell with these Toledan monarchs.' You see, my lord bishop, how the curate of Mediana is more powerful than your lordship, for he has made and unmade kings in three weeks, which you have not accomplished in eight months . . ." (298).

Guevara follows his letter with another to the bishop, who, he has heard, received his first letter with displeasure. Guevara taunts him for the reports that he goes about saying "Is there no one who would catch Master Guevara for me, that I might hang him from a battlement, because he tricked and lured Pedro Girón away from our junta?" (301). "I do not know why you call me a traitor and wish to kill me and hang me from a battlement, for I do not desire to see your lordship hanged but reformed" (302).

Number 49 is in answer to a letter from the rebel leader Juan de Padilla, delivered by his servant. Guevara's reply hints that he and the servant have exchanged secret information relating to the possible defection of Padilla. An eloquent and persuasive letter—whether ever written for delivery in reality or not—which marshals arguments against the commune and adds warnings that, after the sad facts of Padilla's beheading, make emotional reading. Guevara also shows his instinctive horror of popular movements: "I also told you, sir, that what the commoners demanded—that is, that in Castile everyone should contribute, everyone should be equal, everyone should pay taxes, and that they should be governed as in the republics of Italy—... is scandalous to hear and blasphemous to say ..." (305).

Number 51 is a letter to María Pacheco, the heroic wife of Juan de Padilla, who Guevara claims has written him a vitriolic letter because he had tried to persuade her husband by letter to defect from the side of the commune. The friar accuses the lady of unworthy motives: that she dreamed her husband was grand master of the Order of St. James, that she has a crazy slave-woman who predicts that she will be queen of Spain. He taunts her for her show of piety—she wore black—when she robbed the silver from the treasury of the Cathedral of Toledo: "O blessed theft, oh glorious sack, oh fortunate silver, since you were worthy to be stolen with such devotion! ..." (323). And he ends the letter with a perfunctory plea that she cease her activities and surrender Toledo.

Letter 52 is the most controversial piece in the *Familiar Letters,* since it is a speech that Guevara claims to have delivered to an important gathering of rebels. Not only does Guevara reproduce his speech, but he also describes how it was received and includes the replies given to him by the bishop of Zamora and other rebels.

Guevara asserts that he has gone back and forth between the enemy camps seven times, that he has been seized and mistreated, that he has brought an official list of compromises from the governors (the Cardinal Adrian, the future pope, the Admiral of Castile, and the Constable of Castile). He reviews the origins of the rebellion and his own participation as an eyewitness.

Guevara lists the outrages perpetrated by the rebels and deplores their lawlessness; he repeats the reasons given by the rebels for their dissatisfaction, particularly the influx of Flemings, and he reads the list of points on which the royalists are willing to make concessions. He concludes with a dramatic peroration:

If you, sirs, are what you proclaim throughout Castile that you are, to wit, the redeemers of the republic and restorers of the liberty of Castile, behold, we offer you her redemption and indeed her restoration, because so numerous and such excellent things as these you would not think to ask or dare to request. The hour has now arrived, sirs, in which we shall discover whether what you say is one thing and what you desire is another; for if you desire the general good, it is now given to you; if you seek your own interest, it will not be permitted, for, to tell the truth, it is not just but unjust that each should desire to improve his house by the sweat of the wretched republic. In conclusion, here in the church of Villabrájima, for my part, sirs, I beg you on bended knee, and on behalf of the governors I urge you, and on behalf of the king I command you to lay down your arms, to break camp, to surrender Tordesillas; if you do not, from this moment I declare war and I justify the claim of the governors that all the harm and deaths that henceforth may occur in the realm shall be upon your souls and not upon their consciences. (332–33)

At this impassioned close, the friar fell to his knees, amid the clamor, shouting, scoffing, and stamping of the crowd. Two of the rebels courteously helped him to his feet, and the bishop of Zamora—well characterized by the speech which Guevara puts in his mouth—condescendingly and with some humor sends him packing. But the day was not wasted, for Guevara claims that in secret talks with the rebel Don Pedro Girón, Girón agreed to move his camp out of the way so that the governors might march on the town where Queen Joan the Mad was a willing prisoner of the rebels: and "from that expedition our lady the queen was freed and the members of the junta captured" (335).

Having extracted the sermons, the erudite and moral letters, and those which deal with the communes, we are left with what modern readers would probably agree are "familiar" letters, those which at least imitate private correspondence convincingly. They are often humorous; indeed, all of Guevara's works, except the religious ones, are liberally salted with humor. In fact, the occasional sparks of wit are what most charm us in Guevara's writing, though when he points out an anecdote or a retort as being especially witty, we are likely to find it strangely pointless, silly, or even crude. The only letter which he (or his publisher) advertises as funny verges on cruelty (the letter to his niece, whose pet has died). This last category embraces I, 5, 6, 9, 10, 12–14, 17, 26, 36, 38, 39, 41–43, 46, 53, 57, 58, 60, 61, 66–69; and II, 3, 13, 14, 21, 22, 27, 36, 38.

Number 9, from volume I, is a very funny letter to Don Pedro Girón, in which Guevara berates him for his terrible penmanship. Girón's letter, according to the annoyed recipient, was written on coarse paper with pale ink, the lines were uneven, the letters backward, and the words smeared: "either you wrote it by moonlight, sir, or some schoolchild [wrote it]" (68). It was so illegible that the puzzled addressee gave it to various experts in ancient and foreign languages (e.g., Marineo Sículo, a noted humanist and Greek scholar) and to a magician, who put it in a magic circle and assured Guevara that it was not bewitched. "Would to God, sir, that you had been the secretary of Manichaeus, Arrius, Nestorius . . . and indeed of Luther and of all the other heretics that have been in the world, because . . . neither we nor anyone else would have managed to read them" (69). For thousands of years the alphabet has remained unchanged, but "it may be that you have found a new ABC for writing" (70). The letter concludes with court gossip.

Number 10, though the title of the letter indicates that it deals with the brevity of ancient epistles, is really about Guevara's family and his own appearance: "You write, sir, asking why, since I am of so ancient a lineage, so tall, so prolix in the *mementos* of the mass, and so lengthy in preaching, I am so short in writing..." (73). Guevara answers these "questions" in order giving a brief account of his family and its branches. "You also say, sir, that in preaching I am long-winded and tiresome.... I was brought to the emperor's court thirty-eight years ago, during which time I have seen everything grow except sermons, which are unchanged" (77–78).

One of the most interesting of the letters in this group is Number 17, dated 1532. Charles was in Flanders, and the court at Medina del Campo was small and, apparently, rather boring. Guevara blessed the empress' table every day, and he describes her Portuguese protocol: "She eats what she eats cold, in a cold room, alone, in silence, while everyone watches her.... These are five conditions any one of which would be enough to make the meal very unpleasant for me" (115). She eats sparingly of plain food and drinks watery wine. Around her table kneel three ladies-in-waiting who take the dishes from the waiters and cut and serve them to the queen. "All the other ladies are present, standing against the wall, not silent but talking, not alone but in company, so that three of them give the empress something to eat and the rest give the gentlemen something to talk about. The Portuguese manner is dignified and jolly, although in truth sometimes the ladies laugh so much and the gentlemen talk so loud that they lose their dignity and even annoy her Majesty" (117). This letter also illustrates the indifference of Guevara (or his publisher) to the accuracy of the dates. In the body of the letter, Guevara says such things as "the winter is severe" (118), but the letter is dated 18 July.

The third letter in volume II, from the bishop of Palencia, inquires on the correct way to greet and take leave. "It is not one of the small refinements of court to know, depending on one's position, how to bow, how long to remove one's hat, whether to rise from the chair, whether to go out to meet [the visitor] at the door, what to say at the beginning of the conversation so that people may not consider one a poor courtier or accuse one of rudeness. To say *you* (*vos*) to one who deserves *your worship* (*merced*) ... convicts him who writes it or says it of ignorance or reveals him as ill bred" (49). The constant references in later sixteenth- and seventeenth-century litera-

ture to the social difficulties created by the Spanish passion for
titles of respect and by the numerous possible forms of address
makes one understand Jespersen's admiration of the modern
English speaking custom of using the same form for everyone.
Guevara reviews ancient forms of address as well as modern
greetings in Sicilian dialect, Italian, Valencian dialect, and Catalan. "Here in this Castile of ours, the ways and varieties of
greeting and leave-taking and calling to one another are amaz-
ing and even laughable. . . . The style at court is to say *I kiss
your worship's hands*; others say *I kiss your lordship's feet,* [or]
. . . *I am the servant and perpetual slave of your house.* . . . It
embarrasses me to hear *I kiss your hands* and it nauseates me
to hear *I kiss your feet,* because with our hands we wipe our
noses, with our hands we wipe the matter from our eyes, with
our hands we scratch our itch—and we make use of them for
other things which are unmentionable in public. With regard
to the feet, we cannot deny that they are usually sweaty, have
long toenails, are full of callouses, have bunions, and are indeed
covered with dust and loaded with mud" (51–52). Guevara
comments on the hypocrisy of these extravagant greetings and
says that one should use Christ's greeting, *Peace be with you,*
"except that we pride ourselves on being courtiers rather than
Christians" (52).

The thirty-eighth letter of volume II is to a niece "who fell
ill out of sorrow because her little bitch died. It is a courtly letter, written with very amusing words" (405) according to the
epigraph. Perhaps the eccentricities of dog-lovers are peculiarly
Anglo-Saxon; one seems, at least, to see fewer overfed, over-
coddled animals in Hispanic countries; but the amusement of
Guevara and his relatives over their cousin's misery seems cruel
today. To twit her, Guevara indulges in a pedantic joke:
". . . as the divine Plato said, 'he who loves is like what he
loves' . . . [therefore,] if I love a brute, I become a brute; from
which we can infer that since you placed your love on a bitch,
without scruples we can say 'Here, doggy, doggy' to you. . . .
I cannot imagine what you got out of your love for a little
bitch or what recompense she gave you for your love except
covering you with hair, befouling your parlor, sleeping on your
divan, giving you fleas . . ." (408–09). He becomes even more

sarcastic: "What a pity you did not give your little bitch a solemn funeral and call out the Confraternity of Mercy, because if you had, she could have been absolved by papal bull, and all the religious brotherhoods would pray for her" (410). "How careless of you not to have called Mother Gallarda [the midwife] for your bitch's whelping, not to have gone on pilgrimage to St. Christopher, nor to have wrapped St. Quiteria's belt around her because she might have survived the parturition and you might have been spared the weeping" (411). (In Guevara's defense, I remind the reader that he brought a cat from Italy, so he was at least not an animal hater.)

II   *Models and Sources*

Guevara indirectly gives us his "official" models in the *Familiar Letters*. They are Plutarch, Seneca, Plato, Phalaris, and Marcus Aurelius. The works of Plutarch and the Scriptores Historiae Augustae are full of letters which are not historical in our sense of the word but in the sense that they are consistent with what might or should have happened. Such ornaments were considered elegant, entertaining, and legitimate procedures. Plutarch himself has left no correspondence. Plato and Phalaris left no authentic correspondence, but until the eighteenth century, collections of letters attributed to them were popular among scholars. Seneca, of course, left letters which are still much read and admired. In his other works, Guevara frequently mentions the letters of Pliny the Younger and Cicero. The bishop tries to counterfeit classical letters in some cases (epistles attributed to Plutarch and Marcus); in others, he strives to imitate the literary tone, the mixture of universally applicable truths and private allusions found particularly in Pliny and Seneca. Besides the famous classical letter writers, contemporary humanists were publishing their correspondence, and Guevara thereby associates himself with such luminaries as Erasmus.

René Costes states that the letters of Hernando del Pulgar, chronicler of the Catholic Monarchs and Latin Secretary, who published his correspondence in 1486, seem to be the source of some of Guevara's material and certain traits of style: "They are, before the publication of the immense matter of the *Famil-*

iar Letters, the first writing in this genre where the familiar tone is united with a didactic intention" (*Oeuvres,* p. 132). Similarities are Pulgar's insertion of diplomatic speeches, his claims that people seek him out as a correspondent, allusions to favors done by him and acknowledgment of gifts from beneficiaries, the mixture of "doctrine" and humor in imitation of Cicero's *Familiar Letters,* and the display of erudition. Pulgar, following Cicero, writes letters on the disadvantages of old age and to a friend in exile, as does Guevara. And the anecdote of Boabdil, last king of Granada, probably comes from Pulgar. Costes says that the best proof of the similarity is the inclusion of Pulgar's correspondence, without their author's name, in the Italian edition of Guevara's letters. Costes has also documented Guevara's borrowings and adaptations from Aulus Gellius (letters I, 21, 24, 26, 59; and II, 4, 15), notably the versions of Androcles and the lion, and the horse of Sejanus.

The researches of K. A. Blüher into the influence of Seneca in Spain have revealed that the source of letter 21, volume I, on wrath, and letter 43, volume II, on the tribulations of the just, are Seneca's *De ira* and *De providentia.* The second of these two letters, in Latin (and garbled beyond recognition in the Cossío edition), is a cento of quotations from *De providentia,* adapted to Guevara's own style and vaguely attributed to Plato and Demetrius, who is cited by Seneca. All other attributions to Seneca, according to Blüher, are false. It is interesting to note that several English scholars have placed Guevara in the "Senecan" tradition of letter writers who have influenced the epistolary genre in Britain. This Senecan element must be purely formal, since Blüher finds very few points of contact between Stoicism and Guevara's writings, which he considers to be more in the tradition of Christian *contemptus mundi.*[3]

In his original article ("La originalidad renacentista...," *NRFH* 9, no. 2 [1955], 116, n. 5), Juan Marichal suggests that Guevara utilized the Latin letters (1514) and unpublished Spanish correspondence of Dr. Francisco López de Villalobos, an older contemporary who was one of Charles V's physicians. Marichal announced a future study on this subject, but it has never appeared, perhaps because the similarities are not proof of a connection between the two writers.

Fidèle de Ros, in his study of the religious thought of Guevara, examines three of the speeches in part II of the *Familiar Letters* and finds that they draw on Osuna's first, third, and fourth *Alphabets* for ideas and arguments.[4]

III *Forms*

As I have already observed, many of the letters are essays or, as Costes calls them, dissertations on historical, erudite subjects, though they have epistolary form. According to postclassical rhetorical theory, letters were written orations; they therefore follow the precepts of traditional oratory, with its "capturing" of the audience's sympathetic attention, its exposition, divisions, developments, illustrations, and *elegantiae* of language.

The sermons are of special interest. They preserve, at least vestigially, medieval sermon–form, though Guevara's plans are by no means rigid. In the Middle Ages (the thirteenth century, for example), the preacher approached his principal theme by way of a secondary text, called the *prothema*, which supposedly provided a clever introduction to his topic. This introductory portion customarily ended with a prayer. The text that provided the *thema* was often divided and the divisions expounded in order. The sermon also concluded with a prayer. A schematic analysis of epistle number 2 from part II shows this basic structure:

Text. Luke 23. 42: "Lord, remember me when thou comest into thy kingdom." This is stated without comment.

I.   Introduction: brief comment on text of Boethius, "Quod nil ex omni parte beatum."

II. Secondary theme: Psalm 119. 137: "Righteous art thou, O Lord, and upright are thy judgments."
Question: If God is just, why did Jesus take the Good Thief, who had done him no service, to Paradise; why not Judas instead?
Answer: Because God judges men's hearts and because the Good Thief had faith, as he proved when he cried, "Remember me. . . ." (Reintroduction of text).

III. Principal theme: "Remember me. . . ." Development by means of conceits: (1) the Good Thief "stole" Paradise;

(2) the Good Thief gave to Christ all that he had left, his heart and his power of speech (idea taken from St. Gregory the Great, *Morals on the Book of Job*, 18.64); if Christ had followed the urging of the Wicked Thief and had saved himself, there would be no salvation for man.

IV. Theme continued: Luke 23. 40–41: the words of the Good Thief, "Dost not thou fear God? . . ." Development by means of conceits: (1) The Good Thief was the church's first preacher; (2) his "sermon" had six divisions; the meaning of each division.

V. Conclusions: apostrophe to Christ, using the Good Thief's words (i.e., repetition of theme); Christ's words to the Good Thief; brief prayer for God's mercy.

This same kind of organization is apparent in the longer sermons.

Another element of organization used by Guevara in many guises in all of his works is the question-and-answer series. In the letters, most of which are answers to requests for information or advice, there are a number of these exchanges which Guevara once jokingly calls a game of "guess who" ("adevina quién te dio," [II, 174]). In letter number 13, part II, the regent of Naples, Dr. Sumier, asks the bishop some thirty difficult questions: how to choose a friend, what things in life are priceless, what things most easily deceive a man, the qualities of a just judge, etc. Each question begins "You ask me, sir, . . ."; to which Guevara replies, "Answering this, I say that there are four [or some other number], to wit. . . ." These showy parlor games obviously delighted Guevara. They are related to the wisdom literature to which he often turns (e.g., Valerius Maximus, Plutarch's *Apophthegmata*, Diogenes Laertius) and which he often imitates. Usually a sage utters memorable answers to a series of difficult questions.

Costes reminds us that fifteenth-century collections of lyric poetry (*cancioneros*) are sources of similar guessing-games. But the custom had by no means died out in Guevara's day. A fellow Franciscan and almost exact contemporary, Fray Luis de Escobar, published a book of poetic questions and answers in 1550 (but composed mostly in the 1520s and '30s, apparently) addressed to the Admiral of Castile, who asks most of the questions and who, according to Guevara, had also plagued him with impertinent questions. Fr. Escobar's questions deal with scrip-

tural and theological matters, though they wander into rather
remote areas. Question 206, for example, takes up the subject
of Joseph's age when he married Mary.[5]

IV *Contemporary Allusions*

Since the *Familiar Letters* are presumably *all* contemporary,
this may appear to be a superfluous heading. But there are in
fact five "ancient" letters, written perhaps as early as the Commune Rebellion, that, in my opinion, allude to Spanish dissatisfaction with Charles's government of Spain and his foreign policies.

There appear in volume II, without addressee or prefatory
remarks of any kind, five letters (epistles 30 through 34)
exchanged between Plutarch and his former pupil, the new
emperor Trajan, and between Trajan and the Senate. Plutarch's
letter to Trajan, full of solemn advice for the novice ruler, comes
accompanied by a gift: "I have written for you a book *On the
Ancient Republic.* If you profit by what I have written in it
and by what I have said at other times, you will have in me
a crier of your famous acts and a chronicler of your great deeds"
(353–54). To this, Trajan replies, praising the purity of diction
and soundness of reasoning of his teacher's letter, expressing his
humble gratitude. "I write all of this to you, dear teacher, so
that . . . you will counsel me in what I must do and warn me
where I may stumble, for if Rome considers me the defender
of her republic, I consider you the overseer of my life. If I at
any time seem to you to be cross because of your advice or
criticism, I beg you, dear teacher, not to feel pain at my pain,
for in such cases I will not be annoyed because of what you
will have said to me but because of the shame at what I shall
have done" (357). Trajan also writes to the Senate on the
death of Nerva and on his acceptance of the emperorship,
detailing the terrible responsibilities of rulers. In a second letter
to the same body, he confirms their opinion that government
appointments should be annual, not perpetual, to prevent a
bureaucratic pride among entrenched officials. Referring to his
war in Germania, he says: ". . . in good princes, it is a lesser
evil to be careless in matters of war than in the government of

the republic. The prince should remember that they did not choose him to fight but to rule, not to kill enemies, but to extirpate vices; not to go off to war, but to reside in his republic; not to sack anyone's property, but to maintain everyone in justice..." (366).

The Senate answers Trajan's letters reminding him of his grave responsibilities. They allude to his "foreign" origins ("Since you were born in Spain... it may be that, not knowing the laws to which we have sworn and the customs we hold, you may do things to our harm and your disgrace..." [372–73].), to his wars in Germania, to his favoritism ("... if you do not make an effort to love and deal with all equally..." we can never have peace [373].), to the squabbles in the Senate, to Trajan's dubious nominees for offices.

There are interesting parallels between the problems of the young emperor Charles—foreign upbringing, unfamiliarity with Spanish customs and laws, the wars of religion in Germany, his absence from Spain, his Flemish appointees—and the fictitious problems of Trajan. Guevara may be inventing these problems in order to expound universal principles of rulership, but so many points of contact with contemporary problems could hardly be accidental. Guevara himself hides behind the persona of Plutarch, the severe but kindly preceptor who has written a book on rulership in antiquity—a work like *The Golden Book of Marcus Aurelius,* no doubt—because he understands the problems of high office and is sympathetic with its loneliness. One is reminded that he also invented parallels between Charles and Trajan in the *Lives of Ten Emperors.*

To summarize: Guevara, like many a humanist before and after him, was publishing correspondence carefully selected for its variety of styles, its pleasantly diverse contents, its universal ethical values, and—quite obviously—for the flattering light in which it shows the author. Virtually all of the letters are answers to requests for information or advice from famous personages. Those in which the author shows indignation are directed at nonentities or traitors or perhaps friends who were safely in the grave. But there is not a word which shows the author to have any human failings beyond the most harmless impatience.

Consistent with his posture in all of his other works, Guevara presents himself as a much sought-after and respected adviser; he obliquely compares himself with the teachers of Marcus Aurelius and Trajan; he is always the giver of counsel, never the recipient. As a result of this one-sided picture of himself, there is no convincing tone of familiarity in the letters because there is no exchange, real or fictional. But fray Antonio was, after all, a court preacher, priest, and confessor, living in a period when free moral advice flowed copiously from every writer's pen, even when the subject was fiction, and thus the pose of counsellor may be perfectly justified.

V *Pedro de Rúa*

It is convenient to mention here the first of Guevara's two most famous detractors, Pedro de Rúa. (The second was Pierre Bayle.) Rúa was an extremely learned man who taught grammar at Soria and who had known Guevara at Avila when he was prelate of the Franciscan monastery there. They were neighbors and Rúa says that he often visited Guevara. After the publication in 1539 of part I of Guevara's *Familiar Letters* and other works, Rúa wrote to him a series of three letters of devastating criticism (the first extremely polite, the second and third increasingly caustic), in which he identifies errors and fictions and takes the bishop to task for his disservice to historical truth and to his position as an ecclesiastic.[6] Rúa's letters still quiver with the indignation of an honest scholar, scandalized by the bishop's shameless frauds—and no doubt by their success. Guevara answered Rúa after receiving the first two letters. Since Rúa's criticisms are, with a few exceptions, absolutely justified, there was nothing that Guevara could say; so he affects polite indifference: "... I appreciate your first letter and this one; they supplement what little I know and [show] how much I err. You have noted very few things in my scribblings [*obrillas*] [i.e., considering all the errors they no doubt contain], and your suggestions will be helpful in reviewing what I have done and emending what I shall do in the future. As you know, sir, the writers of humane letters are so contradictory [*varios*] that, outside of Holy Scripture, one cannot affirm or deny anything; and to tell the truth, I believe very few of them, except as a source of amusement. . . ."[7] (The vagueness of Guevara's letter makes it difficult to translate.) Rúa's *Letters of Censure,* as the eighteenth-century edition is called, apparently circulated in manuscript (judging by a remark in a letter from Rúa to his acquaintance, Alvar Gómez de Castro, professor of Greek at Alcalá).[8] They were published by Rúa in 1549, ten years after the appearance of the works they censure and four years after Guevara's death, and were not printed again until 1736. The third, and most recent, edition is that of 1850, where they appear in the same volume with Guevara's letters. Modern readers, even scholars, no longer care about the inaccuracy of Guevara's citations, his chronological tangles, or the extent of his distortions of ancient history; they no longer regard extensive knowledge of the classics as the one infallible sign of learning; and they approach Guevara already knowing that he is full of imaginary history. As a result, Rúa's letters seem to be exercises in pedantry. But they have been of great service to modern editors and critics who attempt to pin down Guevara's original contributions, and they are an admirable index of the high professional standards of Spanish humanism of the early sixteenth century.[9]

VI *Guevara and "Authority"*

The most vexing question in the study of Guevara is how to understand his constant use of imaginary "sources." Reaction to Guevara's deceptions has usually been indignant. Pedro de Rúa, the first scholar to study the allusions systematically, wrote to Guevara, as we have seen, that he was betraying his profession as official historian and was, considering his ecclesiastical office, setting a bad example; Pierre Bayle called him a "public poisoner." Modern scholars are more interested in the creative aspect of the bishop's work and therefore are tolerant of the deception—Mrs. Malkiel is an exception here—or they explain it as a function of Guevara's position at court as a "high-born buffoon," to use Costes's words, whom no one took seriously.

It is useful in this connection, I believe, to consider *The Golden Book of Marcus Aurelius* separately from the rest of the bishop's production. *The Golden Book* in its original form is unquestionably a novel, influenced by the form of the then popular fictional biographies of heroes of chivalry (Guevara himself condemns several by name but elsewhere alludes to "the illustrious" Tirante, whom he considers as historical).[10] It is an exemplary substitute for the novels of chivalry, a genre which the Spanish moralists universally detest. Since Guevara was writing a novel, he was free to invent—as did the writers of novels of chivalry, who also purported to be writing "history"— ancient sources, historical figures, and the like. Humanists almost daily discovered some new classical work in the Italian libraries; so Guevara claims to have discovered the lost works of Marcus Aurelius (mentioned by Marcus's real biographers), unknown biographies by Marcus's teachers, etc. All of these trappings give the novel an up-to-date flavor that added to its aura of reality. No one could therefore reasonably object to Guevara's fictionalizing; even Rúa says that he is leaving the *Marcus Aurelius* out of his examination "because I know that your worship considers it sacrosanct, as the Trojans and their *palladium*." If Guevara had never written another word, there would be no difficulty in accepting his forgeries.

But beginning with the enlarged version of *The Golden Book of Marcus Aurelius*, the *Dial of Princes*, Guevara fictionalizes material that is not "novelistic"; and it is in this gray area that the problem of Guevara's integrity as an author arises. All the rest of Guevara's production is suspect because of the impossibility of untangling authentic sources from distorted or invented sources.

It is patently impossible to attribute the really vast amount of fictional quotations, etc., to a fuzzy memory of his wide reading, inaccurate texts, indifference, or—for that matter—to a sinister dishonesty, as various scholars have proposed. I suggest that what explains Guevara's reckless name-dropping (for that is exactly what it is) is the superstitious respect for *auctoritas*—a respect which lasted among educated men until the Romantic period. We have an instructive example of the compelling need to find an "authority" for everything in the official edition of King James I's *Basilikon Doron*, a compilation of commonplaces out of regimens of princes, with the sources indicated in elaborate marginalia. These were prepared by the king and his editors, and in a number of places, where an ancient authority cannot be found to support the king's arguments, the editors (and king?) have invented a suitably impressive one. Since Guevara was himself the source of a number of passages in the *Basilikon Doron,* one may reasonably object that the invented sources (e.g., Demosthenes' *Eighth Philippic*) are to be found buried in the inexhaustible authorities of the *Dial of Princes.* I submit, however, that, if he could not fool a provincial Latin teacher like Pedro de Rúa, the professional humanists employed by the king of England to edit his works would not be gulled by Guevara for long, and that, if the king or his editors let such frauds remain when it would have been perfectly acceptable (to us) to give them no attribution but the king's fertile wit, it is because the desire to find an ancient source for all wise and clever sayings overrode their interest in historical accuracy. If one looks at a contemporary theological treatise or sermon in which the sources are indicated, he will see that what the writer sought was not absolute originality of thought but rather a new and beautiful, or at least edifying, combination of authoritative writings and scriptures. The same is true of nontheological erudite materials, and not infrequently of what we would consider artistic materials. In a somewhat overstated way, one might say that from the sixteenth-century point of view, if something had not been thought or said by the ancients, it probably was not worth thinking or saying. The test of an educated man was his ability to manipulate classical sources or accepted theological works and scripture. And, as if they were compiling legal briefs, humanists piled up authorities for every idea, no matter how trivial. Since we modern readers of Guevara, with the possible exception of priests, have no concept of the stultifying universality of the practice of heaping up authorities, and since we read only selected examples of sixteenth-century imaginative literature (which were remarkable in their own day), we have difficulty in appreciating the pressure of habit exerted on an author like Guevara.

I suggest that Guevara experimented with the technique of mixing real and imaginary authorities in the first version of the novel and found it so successful that he later used it even in his sermons and ascetic works, where ethics, not dogma, is the issue. If the *Marcus Aurelius* is not a "serious" work, the *Dial of Princes* and all subsequent writings are; and all serious works were invariably accompanied by the ponderous apparatus of authorities.

Though Guevara was not much of a Latin scholar, he could certainly make out the drift of most of the works he cites, and he had at his disposal translations of a great many of the standard works of antiquity and the Middle Ages which are often named in his writings. If he had been really interested in making a reputation for himself as a scholarly churchman who chose to write in Spanish because it reached a wider audience, he could have done so without undue effort. (Lope de Vega is an interesting case of such pretentiousness.)

Guevara betrayed contemporary humanistic feeling for the sacredness of authority by applying the rules of the game of fiction to "serious" literature like classical biography, archaeology, or moral essays. Rúa makes this quite clear in his last letter.

Guevara's careful obfuscations are his "gimmick" to attract the special reader of the second quarter of sixteenth-century Spain. He must have felt that his moral intention justified what even today seems a questionable procedure; his last works, intended for his monks, are as full of misleading and fictional religious material as his earlier works are full of imaginary classical material. He obviously made no distinction between religious and nonreligious writing, though we usually think that a Spanish churchman would be the last to tamper with such dangerous matter. But even in the *Monks' Chapel* (*Oratorio de religiosos*), Guevara's intentions are not dogmatic. In fact, the Inquisition later took exception to two or three expressions in the *Oratorio,* which were expunged in late sixteenth-century editions, but *not* to the false attributions to such doctors of the church as St. Augustine or St. Bonaventure.

Guevara was not a cynic in spite of his letter to Rúa. Cynics do not write thousands of pages of moral precepts. He was not a neurotic ignoramus who spent twenty years trying to pass himself off as a scholar. What would be the point after the publication of *The Golden Book,* when everyone knew that the "rediscovered" documents were imaginary? If any further proof were needed that it was not the discovery of Guevara's frauds which led to his decline in popularity, consider the incredible efforts of Johannes Wanckelius, a German scholar of fabulous erudition, who in the early seventeenth century translated Guevara's *Dial of Princes* into Latin, locating most of the authentic sources and using the wording of the original where possible, as well as adding several thousand marginal glosses in Greek, Latin, German, Spanish, and French, in which he presents parallel texts when he cannot locate an authority for the exact citation. Guevara must have had a strong attraction indeed to merit such a labor of love. The proofreading alone would discourage a modern scholar.[11]

CHAPTER 9

The Monks' Chapel *and* The Mount of Calvary, *Parts I and II*

I N 1542, Father Guevara published the first of three long
religious works which were relatively popular in the sixteenth
and seventeenth centuries but which have disappeared like most
of the innumerable devotional and ascetic books of the period,
even from the most scholarly reading lists. It is also the only
one to be reprinted since the eighteenth century: *Oratorio de
religiosos y ejercicio de virtuosos*[1] (roughly translated as *The
Monks' Chapel and Spiritual Exercises for the Virtuous*).[2] It
was never englished, so I shall call it the *Oratorio* for convenience' sake.

I *Contents of the* Oratorio

The *Oratorio* consists of a prologue and fifty-six chapters
(one misnumbered). It has almost none of the autobiographical
elements which enliven the letters, for example, and it has even
less of their easy humor. The tone is uniformly magisterial and
solemn, though rather friendly. Its principal interest lies in the
additional light it casts on the literary methods of its author
and in the glimpse it affords of sixteenth-century monastic life.
The work is addressed to the reader, who is presumed to be
a monk, whom the author calls "Brother," "Father," etc., though
he is not consistent.

One may say broadly that the *Oratorio* discusses the charac-
teristics and activities of the good monk: gratitude to God for
having called him to a monastic life, obedience, control of his
tongue, abstemiousness, diligence in the choir and in prayer,
detachment from worldly possessions, chastity, patience in in-
firmity, and perseverance. There are also several chapters on

prelacy and its special burdens. Guevara tends to group the chapters according to their contents: for example, 15–18 on prelacy; 19–21 on the evils of idle talk; 24–33 on abstinence, fasting, the dangers of eating outside the monastery, and table manners; 34–40 on the divine office and prayer; 41–45 on obedience; 46–48 on possessions; 49–50 on chastity: In general, the bishop follows his by now well-established technique of emphasizing the negative aspects of existence, of the "pointless activity" (*bullicios*) of the world—in short, the "thou shalt not" side of Christian asceticism.

In his chats with his monasic reader, Fr. Guevara gives us, unintentionally, a description of ordinary men trying to live up to the exalted religious ideal of monasticism but held down by the temptations, quirks, and petty difficulties of human existence. A few examples will illustrate the confidential tone of the *Oratorio*: "Tell me, I beg you, why laymen, when they meet us, commend themselves to our prayers, tip their hats to us, kiss our hands, and show us such respect, if not because they think that we are saints and that through our merits they will be saved? If those who live in the world could see how distracted our thoughts are and how aimlessly we wander through the monasteries, do you believe, Brother, that they would give us what they give us and would think of us as they do?" (464).

On unworthy motives: "... not all those who come to take the habit come guided by the Holy Spirit, since we see that some come because they have been humiliated in the world, others because they have no money, others because they have committed some misdeed, others because they were too easygoing, and even others who were too foolish and simple for the world ... they have not rejected the world, but the world them. The prelate, who represents the Lord, must not permit the religious life to be the dungheap of the world, when the world should be the dungheap of the religious life..." (493).

In a time when an estimated third of the population of the Peninsula was directly connected with the church either as ecclesiastics or as functionaries (such as canon lawyers, custodians, etc.), it is easy to see that a large number, if not a large percentage, of the religious would be unhappy with a life which it was almost impossible to leave without disgrace:

"There are many monks who do not dare to run away out of shame, but who apostasize in their consciences, which engenders laziness in the Order, taking the monk out of the choir, keeping him away from the oratory, resisting the prelate, wandering about the monastery, chatting with those who are at home, and even gossiping about those who are away. Tell me, I pray, which is the worse apostate, he who leaps the monastery walls or he whose body is in the choir but, on the other hand, whose heart is in the world?" (542–43).

One of the most curious chapters in the book is 29, "On the modesty and good manners which the religious must display when he eats outside the monastery." Among the rules of etiquette are the following: "Do not wipe your hands on the tablecloth; do not lick your fingers; do not blow your nose on the napkins; do not scratch your neck at the table; do not eat with both cheeks full, like a monkey; do not fill your soup-plate with sops or knock bones [against the table] in order to extract the marrow..."(614). Take special care not to make idle chatter at table or take part in gossip. If women are present, avoid talking to them, though they will look you over from head to toe. "Do not put a bib under your chin, like an old man; do not drape the napkin over your shoulder like a courtier.... To put three fingers in the dish is considered vulgar, not to take salt with your knife is considered crude..." (615).

A striking proof of the millennial stability of monastic life and, likewise, of the enduring nature of its problems, is the famous eighteenth-century novel *Fray Gerundio de Campazas*, by the Spanish Jesuit José Francisco de Isla. This novel satirizes, among other things, the antiquated style of preaching which emphasized a complicated, showy vocabulary rather than clarity and communication. In order to explain this abuse, Isla writes the imaginary biography of a young monk—the order is not identified, but several orders, including the Franciscans, thought that they were the butt of the satire—who is accepted by his order without proper examination, is not adequately disciplined or trained, and who, from the misguided kindness of some of his superiors and the self-interest of others, is not only permitted to take vows but allowed to preach. Guevara's chapters in the *Oratorio* on the examination of postulants and on the training of young monks might have served as an inspiration for Isla (chapter VI and ff.).[3]

Moved by charity or constrained by importunity, prelates often receive into the order novices who have neither the knowledge to preach nor the devotion to pray, nor the strength to work, nor even the sense to behave themselves; from which many annoyances result for them later, and uproars are engendered in the monasteries. . . . When we say that they should receive unlettered, simple men into the order, it must be understood that their simplicity must be gentle and discreet and dovelike so that they understand what they are vowing and do as they are told; let prelates beware of admitting to the order him who, in the guise of simplicity and sincerity, may make up in cunning what he lacks in discretion. The prelate who receives into the order one who is obviously ignorant and stupid, whose relatives perchance took him to the monastery not so that he might better serve the Lord there but that they might rid themselves of him and unburden themselves of him, is to be blamed. . . . The monk who is not devout or who is not discreet cannot endure the monastery for long, and if he perseveres, he will cause an uproar in the order, because there is nothing more pernicious for religious orders than when an ignorant man arms himself with cunning. (494–95)

II *Sources of the* Oratorio

In 1938, Fr. Fidèle de Ros published a splendid, indignant article on Guevara as an author of ascetic treatises, in which he studies the sources and method of composition.[4] He found that in the *Oratorio*, there are "entire pages borrowed from the *Letters*, and around six of its chapters reproduce verbatim long extracts from the *Favored Courtier*. Furthermore, chapter 4 of the *Oratorio* is a compilation of passages taken from the *Marcus Aurelius*, the *Favored Courtier*, and from the *Dispraise of Court*" (341). "The *Oratorio* is, to a very great extent—about sixteen chapters out of fifty-six—the reedition of passages and even of whole chapters borrowed from the earlier works of the writer himself" (355).

Fr. Ros's catalog of self-plagiarisms produces some interesting facts, though they are not surprising: in a number of the self-borrowings, Guevara copies himself verbatim and then attributes the passage to some famous pagan or Christian writer.

Most of the other attributions, as one would expect, are virtually impossible to verify. Fr. Ros seethes with indignation when discussing Guevara's invention of patristic texts: "At the beginning of modern times, pious fraud, having edification as its goal, was still regarded as legitimate in certain *milieux* ... [but] one hesitates to believe, in spite of everything, that a monk, a bishop could amuse himself for no apparent reason by fabricating [quotations] from St. Augustine or St. Jerome out of whole cloth" (356). In fact, Fr. Ros so detests Guevara that he can find no logical reason for the numerous editions and continued popularity of Guevara's books, which were mere "elementary" treatises of religious discipline.

III *Contents of* The Mount of Calvary

Guevara's last works were *The Mount of Calvary* (1545) and an unfinished book on the Seven Last Words published in 1549, four year after his death, by an anonymous Franciscan editor, with the title *Part II of the Book Called The Mount of Calvary.* Guevara probably intended to publish the books together, since the first edition known (Valladolid, 1545) states on the title page that "the second part of this book ... is in press."[5]

The Mount of Calvary contains fifty-eight chapters, some of them subdivided, on the Passion and Entombment of Christ, a long prologue, a table of contents, and a table of scriptures cited in the work. To the modern reader, the most noticeable characteristic of these meditations is the "abuse of allegorical commentaries," to use Fr. Ros's uncomplimentary phrase. The *figurae* now seems quaint at best and preposterous at worst, as evidenced in the following examples: the reed which the Roman soldiers put into Jesus' hand is a *figura* of the Old Law, because the reed and the altar of the Tabernacle were both hollow; the meditation on the purple robe leads Guevara to discuss prophetic texts in Isaiah on the crushing of grapes and an elaborate comparison between the church and the vine, the faithful and the grapes, the vat and the Passion, the press and the cross, the pressing stone and the Holy Sepulchre, the grape-treader and Christ, and so on. Besides these scriptures interpreted *moraliter*, there are all of the other tricks of the preacher's craft: paraphrasing of the scripture, derivation of words, unsuspected parallels, modern instances, examples from ancient history, biblical and classical archaeology, and hundreds of citations from the church fathers, the saints, and interpretative works like the *Glossa Ordinaria.*

In order to heighten the emotional tone of the work, Guevara is very liberal with apostrophes addressed to the reader (often to "My Brother" or "Brother Prelate"), to the biblical personage in question, or to inanimate objects like Calvary: "O glorious garbage-dump of Calvary, oh rotten dungheap of Golgotha, where but on you did we see the Giver of Life end His life, and where but there and on you did we see death die with His death?" (54 r, v).[6] The "very sorrowful oration by the author" which ends the book is virtually one long apostrophe.

Perhaps the most remarkable example of Guevara's affective devices is his use of dialogue. Just as he amplified or deduced speeches for his historical and fictional characters, so he writes a pathetic dialogue for a very detailed *Pietà* tableau. Joseph of Arimathaea, Nicodemus, and John the Evangelist all speak to the Virgin, who holds the body of Jesus in her lap, asking her to allow them to take her son to be buried. St. Bernard and St. Anselm (or so it was thought) had both written such dialogues in Latin.

IV   *Contents of* The Mount of Calvary, Part II

For part II, the bishop had planned to write a series of "muy devotas contemplaciones" on the Last Words of Jesus, but he completed only "the first five" of them, according to the anonymous prologuer. Since all of the meditations are obviously by Guevara, however, this seems on examination to mean that he more or less completed all but the third and the last word. Of the seventh word, there are four very short sermons which have nothing to do with *In manus tuas,* ("Into Thy hands . . ."), though it would have been a very simple matter for the editor to connect them with the theme with only slight additions. The Third Word (*Mulier ecce filius tuus,* "Woman, behold thy son . . .") is in reality a series of homilies on the mutual love of Jesus and his mother, the prophetic words of Simeon, and

other subjects related to the Blessed Virgin; it has nothing to do
with the stated topic. A number of chapters in the Fifth (*Sitio*,
"I thirst") and Sixth Word (*Consummatum est*, "It is finished")
have no obvious, or have only the most superficial, relation to
the theme, usually in the last line (e.g., 3–4 in the Fifth and 2
and 7 in the Sixth).

Besides the prologue, part II also contains seven "arguments"
at the beginning of each Word by don Pero Vélez de Guevara,
the bishop's socially prominent cousin, son of the count of Oñate.
He is one of the illustrious persons mentioned in the *Familiar
Letters* (I, letters 10 and 64). (Francesillo de Zúñiga calls him
the bishop's "brother," so perhaps they were closer than we have
hitherto believed.) The arguments are short meditations which
do not summarize the following chapters, as one might suppose,
though each deals with some aspect of the seven last words.
They are heavily laced with Latin scriptures, move quickly from
one subject to another, and give the impression of coming from
the pen of a somewhat pompous amateur who has little practice
in writing.

The prologue contains interesting biographical and critical
observations worth quoting:

I beg you, Christian reader, to contemplate and understand in
Christian fashion the spiritual fruit and universal profit that the most
reverend lord Don Antonio de Guevara, bishop of Mondoñedo, has
produced in God's church with his teachings and his books and, you
will say (unless I am deceived), with the truth. . . . And although he
has written all of them in a pleasing style, with great brilliance of
imagination and very exalted doctrine, yet in this last book . . . which
he wrote at the end of his days and in his old age, he exceeded the
others in devotion and fertility of *sententiae*. . . . The lord bishop set
himself to write this work so late in life that he died after he had
finished his first five words, before he could complete the last two.
But the beginnings of them are of such excellence and brilliance . . .
that even he who is not very clever will understand. . . . (ff. 4v–5r)

[While he was writing part II,] how many times was he found bathed
in tears, his pen motionless in his hand, his eyes on the crucifix! Oh
how often were moans and sobs heard while he was writing this work!
Oblivious to himself, forgetful of bodily sustenance and of the other
unavoidable needs of the human body, [he was] completely oblivious

and absorbed and altogether transported by these Seven Words. . . .
One may piously believe that he has great glory and a shining crown
in paradise. . . . (f. 6r)

The style and method of these meditations are similar to those
found in his other devotional writings, so they need no further
comment. The *declaraciones* of Scripture are exceptionally farfetched, however, though one is always on shaky ground in
matters of scriptural allegory: even the silliest and most trivial
interpretations may have very distinguished pedigrees. Perhaps
the most idiotic in part II concerns a passage from Leviticus in
which offerings of fried pastry are dragged into the meditations
on *Consummatum est.* Jesus fried our sins (along with his
tender limbs) with the oil of his love in the frying pan of the
cross (chapter VII of the last word).

There are few of the allusions to human foibles or current
problems[7] that enliven Guevara's other works, and I think that
The Mount of Calvary, especially part II, has aged less grace-
fully than any of the bishop's works.

V   *Sources of Part II*

Fr. Ros has discovered in his examination of the sources that
part II contains numerous borrowings from the work of another
Franciscan and contemporary of Guevara, fray Pedro de Osuna.
As observed above, Osuna was the author of a much admired
series of five devotional books which he called *Alphabets.* Guevara borrows freely from the first and third of these treatises.
But instead of acknowledging them or even of using them
without attribution, he attributes them to St. Ambrose, St. Jerome, and other more prestigious writers of Christian antiquity
or the Middle Ages. Ros's annoyance at Guevara's dishonesty
is boundless: "The pleasant and easy art of appearing erudite
at little expense!" (384).[8] As in the *Oratorio,* there are many
passages clipped out of the *Letters* and revised slightly, sometimes with imaginary attributions. The patristic and pagan
sources show nothing new.

If one remembers that such works as *The Mount of Calvary*
were valued by contemporaries as a basis for meditation, as a
starting point for pondering the "mysteries" of the scriptures

and their applicability, not for originality, then one is in a better position to judge the merits of such antiquated material, which we normally do not consider as "literature." Guevara was (naturally) perfectly aware that originality in interpretation was virtually impossible, but that the faithful needed the constant, repetitious examination of the same passages in many different lights, which helped squeeze every drop of meaning from them: "Granted that many have interpreted this glorious figure [Noah's ark] very thoroughly, still, let us see if we cannot find some other mysteries in it" (223v).

It is important to keep in mind that these works were intended to be read in small, unified portions, and that most people probably heard rather than read them. They are the sort of material that provided the daily readings in monastic refectories. Taken, therefore, in the traditions of vernacular ascetic literature, biblical exegesis, sermons, and other forms which we have long since allowed to die, *The Mount of Calvary* shows up favorably. The rhetoric is masterly, and some of the passages are as exalted and dramatic as any contemporary sermon I am familiar with. The auditory elements, for which Guevara was famous, are handled with great sensitivity and skill. A good preacher could make these old pages come to life. What is gone forever is our capacity to respond to the allusions, the grandiloquence, the microscopic examination of texts in search of correspondences between the Old and New Testaments. And of course we find Guevara's fanciful erudition and plagiarisms distasteful, however worthy the end.

VI *Criticism*

Francisco Márquez Villanueva, who considers the religious treatises as "indispensable" to the understanding of Guevara's works, has written the only critical study to date which deals entirely with their aesthetic value, not their sources.

He suggests that modern critics (and even certain contemporaries like Rúa) have completely misunderstood the literary efforts of Guevara because they have insisted on considering him a moralist, whereas he is an artist, unconcerned with morality or any other extraliterary considerations.

Márquez avers that the satirical element in Guevara's *Oratorio* is more prominent than Ros or other students have conceded. While not Erasmist, it is "a kind of report . . . on the vices and dangers of the cloister, which reveals its imperfections better than any accusation of a more theoretical type" (36). It impresses Márquez as a literary exercise with monastic life as its theme. "What gives the book its special character is the systematic presence of an esthetics of degradation . . . which takes pleasure in bringing monastic life down to the level of stylized caricature . . ." (37). Guevara takes "malicious delight" in depicting the foibles of monks in "picaresque" fashion; he is, indeed, "the spiritual father of the picaresque" (37).

Speaking of the *Monte Calvario*, Márquez says, "The Passion gradually emerges as a bourgeois story, [comprising] a sequence of events seen in their most humdrum aspect and feelings projected on an unheroic scale. The untimely recurrence of the theme of money is characteristic and deliberate, and it reveals a search for humorous effects at any cost, even if it means showing the august protagonists of the Passion in an unflattering light" (40). Guevara "enjoys" the humiliations, the "sadism" of details of the crucifixion; he reduces theological questions to crude analogies (e.g., the comparison of Christ with a man who is injured while trying to stop a fight between God and humankind). Márquez senses ". . . the underlying presence of an effort . . . to break away from the Gospels, to 'de-theologize' the life of Christ in order to present it to us limited to its human facets. . . . In short, what interests Guevara are the great possibilities of the *novel* of the life of Christ. A novel, in this case, *cheap* and antiheroic, somewhat after the fashion of the picaresque. It is precisely this tendency toward pure fiction that engenders whatever is new and valuable in *The Mount of Calvary*" (44) There is likewise a systematic hispanicizing of the action. "In reality, [the religious writings] were not read as edifying matter but as entertainment-literature, like Guevara's other works . . . the fantasies about the life of Christ are identified with those found in the history of Marcus Aurelius" (46).

Guevara is the first case of an "officially erudite author" who, while not parodying the doctrinal treatise, tries to make the reader laugh; he is the first modern European author to attempt to raise humor to the "highest level of literary dignity without ulterior object" (48). Undoubtedly, the seed of this special humor is the medieval preachers' custom of using jokes and tales to amuse the congregation; Guevara influenced preaching in an undesirable way by perpetuating "the worst degenerations" of late medieval preaching. In his religious works, he frequently nullifies the religious value of a passage by glossing insignificant passages from the Old Testament and then adding an ironical twist that deflates it, though the jokes all spring from the ancient practices of biblical exegesis. But he "elevates and rescues a medieval minor genre in order to place it on a plane of artistic dignity, in which the old defects are transformed into attractions of rare charm" (55).[9]

Afterword

SCHOLARS always have so obvious a bias in favor of the literary figures they adopt that it makes their judgments suspect. The reader may therefore be expected to doubt my impartiality. But I think that recent publications on Guevara and his work, after a lapse of twenty years, warrant my saying that the famous bishop of Mondoñedo is now coming into his own. I am inclined to believe that the cause is not, as one might think, significantly better literary historians but the interesting changes in the direction of the contemporary novel and the curious parallels which "new" techniques have with picaresque, chivalrous, and Guevarian prose. Until recently, Guevara's reputation as a pious fraud has been an embarrassment to Spaniards, who either (like Herrera, the famous commentator of Garcilaso) repudiate him outright or else make light of his not inconsiderable talents. Besides the prejudice against him, there are the obstacles to appreciation created by his intimidating bulk, the rarity of such fundamental texts as the *Dial of Princes*, and the consequent dearth of good editions and studies.

The appearance of student editions of the *Letters* and *A Dispraise of the Courtier's Life* and the studies by Grey and Márquez Villanueva are, I think, hopeful signs of new interest in the texts and a more balanced assessment of Guevara's contribution. Doctoral candidates are preparing dissertations at Princeton (an edition of the *Dial*), Wisconsin (a study of the *Letters*), and the University of Cincinnati. The French scholar Augustin Redondo has announced a forthcoming book on Guevara, and I have corresponded with a Scottish linguist interested in the influence of Guevara in that ancient kingdom. In a word, Guevara's stocks are rising. I hope that this study may contribute to the international effort to restore fray Antonio to his proper niche in the pantheon of European letters.

Notes and References

For a list of the standard abbreviations of titles of scholarly journals used in these notes, see the Secondary Sources listed in the Selected Bibliography.

Chapter One

1. J. Gibbs, *Vida de fray Antonio de Guevara (1481–1545)* (Valladolid: Editorial Miñón, 1960), p. 10.

2. See A. Redondo, "Un conseiller de Charles-Quint, ancien boursier du Collège Espagnol Saint-Clément de Bologne: le docteur Fernando de Guevara (1485?–1556)," and J. R. Jones, "El doctor Hernando de Guevara, del Consejo de Su Majestad," both in *El Cardenal Albornoz y el Colegio de España*, II ([Bologna?], 1972), 275–93 and 295–307. Studia Albornotiana, XII.

3. *Libro primero de las epístolas familiares*, ed. José María de Cossío (Madrid: Aldus, 1950–1952), I, 74.

4. The illegitimacy of the father of Antonio and Fernando would supposedly explain certain original traits of the personality of Antonio as it is revealed in his writings. In 1945, Américo Castro analyzed Guevara's work for what it reveals about his personality and found that his style "is the direct expression of his otherwise frustrated life." Castro's thesis is that Guevara's unattainable, neurotic desire for worldly success taught him to use writing as a means of revenge on the one hand and as a way to achieve a kind of imaginary importance on the other. Castro was unaware of the possible illegitimacy of Guevara's father.

In 1951, J. Gibbs republished the sections of a genealogy of the Guevara family which deals with the marriages and offspring of Beltrán. He cautiously offered the idea that Antonio's "conspicuous lack of progress" at court might be explained by his unfortunate birth, especially in view of Queen Isabel's "well-known high standard of morality" (*MLR* 46 [1951], 253–55).

Following the lead of Castro in stylistic analysis and using the data in Gibbs's article, Juan Marichal published four years later another long study, "La originalidad renacentista en el estilo de Guevara," in which he states that the shameful circumstances of the birth of

151

Antonio's father prove "the interpretation of Américo Castro with regard to the 'inferiority complex' of the author of the *Epístolas familiares*."

In 1950, Leo Spitzer had already published a criticism of Castro's article. Spitzer's essay shows that "even if the empirical biography of an author of the sixteenth century revealed to us the existence of 'complexes' and 'repressions,' such a thing in no way means that these complexes are translated directly into his style or that he has adapted the traditional stylistic forms to his complexes (which, in the case of Guevara, seems to be Castro's idea)."

A sort of compromise is reached in Marichal's study, in which Castro's ideas are supposedly vindicated by Gibbs's discovery of the illegitimacy of Guevara's father, while Spitzer's notions about the influence of traditional rhetoric are softened. (Spitzer's article is never mentioned, however.) See the Secondary Sources in the Selected Bibliography for exact references to these articles.

5. *Menosprecio de corte y alabanza de aldea*, ed. M. Martínez de Burgos (Madrid: Espasa-Calpe, 1952 [1914]), p. 10.

6. Lino G. Canedo, "Fray Antonio de Guevara, Obispo de Mondoñedo," *Archivo ibero-americano* 6, nos. 22–23 (1946), 317.

7. Henry Seaver, in *The Great Revolt in Castile* (Boston and New York: Houghton Mifflin, 1928), p. 374, notes that the official correspondence of the Admiral of Castile, one of the three regents who carried on the war for Charles, is "astonishingly ornate, both in rhetorical question, allusion, and antithesis," and Marichal astutely suggests that Guevara might in fact have been the author of the letters, which a contemporary described ironically as "more elegant than Seneca's or Cicero's." See Marichal, *Voluntad del estilo*, 2nd ed., p. 225. This suggestion has interesting ramifications, one of which is that it might explain Guevara's court appointments.

8. *The Great Revolt in Castile*, pp. 212, 364–66. See also Joseph Pérez, "Le 'Razonamiento' de Villabrágima," *BH*, 67, nos. 3–4 (1965), 217–24. This is a very well documented article which finds no trace of Guevara's embassies or his speech in contemporary accounts. At the time when, according to Guevara, he was active as a mediator, the bishop of Cuenca, Diego Ramírez de Villaescusa, made an effort to reconcile the factions—an effort which failed and ruined the bishop's reputation with the anti-*comunero* party. Pérez suggests that Guevara attributed the mediation to himself knowing that the bishop of Cuenca would have no interest in reviving a subject which had brought him exile and political difficulties. (Is it possible that Guevara was a member of Bishop Ramírez' party, one of the "four consellors" mentioned by Peter Martyr? See p. 222, n. 15.)

9. Paul Merimée, "Guevara, Santa Cruz, et le 'razonamiento de Villabrájima,'" *Hommage á Ernest Martinenche: Études hispaniques et américaines* (Paris: Éditions d'Artrey, n.d. [1939?]), pp. 466–67.

10. Angel Uribe, "Guevara, inquisidor del Santo Oficio," *Archivo ibero-americano* 6, nos. 22–23 (1946), 198. Details of Guevara's activities in Valencia and later at the examination of Erasmus's works are found in Uribe's essay.

11. Joseph R. Jones, "Fragments of Antonio de Guevara's Lost Chronicle," *SP* 63 (1966), 30–50. See also Seaver, p. 364, n. 3, and p. 373, n. 6; and Francisco Márquez Villanueva, *Fuentes literarias cervantinas* (Madrid: Gredos, 1973), p. 221, n. 69. Márquez interprets Jones's findings in a different light.

12. See Marcel Bataillon, *Erasmo en España* (Mexico: Fondo de Cultura Económica, 1950), pp. 264–65.

13. Uribe, "Guevara, inquisidor . . . ," 263–68.

14. René Costes, *Antonio de Guevara: Son Oeuvre* (Paris and Bordeaux: E. de Boccard; Feret et fils, 1926). Bibliothèque de l'École des Hautes Études Hispaniques, Fascicule X, 2. According to Costes (pp. 4 ff.), the three "clandestine" editions were authorized by Guevara.

15. Ramón Menéndez Pidal, "Idea imperial de Carlos V," in *Idea imperial de Carlos V*, 2nd ed. (Mexico: Espasa-Calpe: B.A., 1943), pp. 27–28. Colección Austral 172.

Américo Castro, *"El villano del Danubio" y otros fragmentos* (Princeton: Princeton University Press, 1945), p. xx, believes that an earlier speech of June, 1528, as well as a speech before the pope in 1536 are also by Guevara. Marichal, *Voluntad*, p. 255, suggests (as is noted above) that Guevara also composed proclamations for don Fadrique Enríquez.

16. Alonso de Santa Cruz, *Crónica del Emperador Carlos V* (Madrid: Imprenta del Patronato de huérfanos de intendencia e intervención militares, 1922), III, 260.

17. Américo Castro, *Antonio de Guevara: El villano del Danubio y otros fragmentos* (Princeton: Princeton University Press, 1945), p. xx.

18. Francisco Márquez Villanueva, "Fray Antonio de Guevara o la ascética novelada," *Espiritualidad y literatura en el siglo XVI*, (Madrid-Barcelona: Alfaguara, 1968), p. 29, n. 11: "It is certain that Guevara must have fallen into something like disfavor with the emperor. A comparison of Guevara's activities at court up to 1530 . . . with the solitude of his last years in his wretched diocese of Mondoñedo, which must have been more or less equivalent to exile, leaves no room for doubt. . . ." It seems to me that Márquez does not give sufficient importance to Guevara's activities with the expedition to

Tunis, the speech before the pope, or the appointment to Mondoñedo
—leaving out of consideration the incredible multiplication of the emperor's problems, his extended absences, and so on. Perhaps a
"wretched" bishopric seems a poor accomplishment to moderns, but
for Guevara to have achieved a title, even such a modest one, must
have given him *some* satisfaction (and status) in the Spain of the
Reformation era. Costes, Castro, Márquez, and even Gibbs have, I
think, made too much of his failures and not enough of his social
achievements, however undramatic.

19. For criticism of Guevara's financial practices during his episcopacy, see María Rosa Lida de Malkiel, "Fray Antonio de Guevara:
Edad media y siglo de oro español," *RFH* 7 (1945), 348.

20. The text of Guevara's two wills is found in Lino G. Canedo,
"Fray Antonio de Guevara, obispo de Mondoñedo," *Archivo Ibero-
americano* 6, nos. 22–23 (1946), pp. 316–30.

Chapter Two

1. Numbers in parentheses refer to the edition of the *Libro áureo*
published by R. Foulché-Delbosc in the *Revue Hispanique* 76, no.
169 (1929), 6–319. It is the only modern edition.

2. Laurence Sterne, *Tristram Shandy*, Volume VI, chapter V.

3. *The Scriptores Historiae Augustae*, trans. David Magie (London: William Heineman; N.Y.: G. P. Putnam's Sons, 1921–1932),
Loeb Classical Library, I, xxciii–xxix. The abbreviation *SHA* refers
to this work, page numbers to volume I of the Magie translation.

4. Marcelino Menéndez Pelayo, *Orígines de la novela*, 2nd ed.
(Madrid: CSIC, 1962), II, 119.

5. Guevara also takes details from Politian's translation of Herodian
of Antioch's Roman history, from Eutropius's *Breviarium*—he names
both authors—and from a translation of Cassius Dio Cocceianus's
Roman history, presumably that published in 1526 by Leoniceno.

6. See Menéndez Pelayo, *Orígines*, II, 113–15.

7. It is impractical to make a detailed comparison of the real biography of Marcus Aurelius with Guevara's fiction. The best account,
which I believe contains every known historical fact about Marcus,
with its source, is L.S. Le Nain de Tillemont, *Histoire des Empéreurs
. . .* (Paris, 1700–38). The interested reader may see for himself at
a glance how little historical material Guevara actually uses.

8. Castro, *El villano del Danubio y otros fragmentos*, p. xv.

9. Prudencio de Sandoval, *Historia de la vida y hechos del empera-
dor Carlos V . . .* (Madrid: Ediciones Atlas, 1955–56), I, 85. For
Sandoval's remarks on the corruption and favoritism in Charles's
Flemish officials (which Guevara had seen), see pp. 109–11.

Stephen Gilman believes that the story of the Jew refers to the severity of the Inquisition in its dealings with Jewish converts. He bases his theory on the double meaning of certain phrases and the possible allusion to a notoriously cruel inquisitor named Lucero. These hints, however, do not appear in *The Golden Book*, but in the revisions of *The Dial of Princes*, and without them, there is no indication that the first original speech of the Jew is anything but a condemnation of governor-judges whose lives are examples of immorality, who use their offices to enrich themselves, and whose arbitrary judgments keep the people stirred up to the point of rebellion. See "The Sequel to 'El villano del Danubio,' " *RHM* 31 (1965), 174–84.

10. The *Crónica de don Francesillo de Zúñiga*, in *Curiosidades bibliográficas*, vol. 36 of the *Biblioteca de autores españoles* (Madrid: Atlas, 1950). The chronicle, which covers the years 1516 to 1529, uses outstanding events like the war of the communes as a skeleton on which to hang the absurdities dreamed up by Francesillo in order to mention as many aristocrats as possible. Inclusion is undoubtedly a sign of social prominence, and Guevara's name appears several times (pp. 20, col. b; 27 b[?]; 36 b, 38 a, 52 b twice, 53 a). Francesillo parodies Guevara's elaborate apparatus and his citations (e.g., 13 a, 22 b). Chapter 84, "Concerning a monstrosity which appeared in a cave at the time, and the great wonders and horrors and things that were seen there," is a parody of *The Golden Book*, chapter 26, "Concerning a very frightful monster which was seen in Sicily in the days of the emperor Marcus Aurelius, and the harm which it caused in Palermo." Guevara is mentioned three times in the chapter. See Márquez, *Fuentes literarias cervantinas*, p. 230 and p. 230, n. 85, for a different interpretation.

11. Márquez believes that Guevara was the first European author to write for the nonscholarly reader who wanted entertainment and not instruction. Perhaps our views are not so dissimilar as it might seem, if one considers the Spanish aristocrats and bourgeois readers of Guevara, who were not very numerous after all, as "mass readers," in Márquez's sense of the term. See Márquez, *Fuentes literarias cervantinas*, pp. 191–92.

12. See Augustin Redondo, "Une source du 'Libro de la vida y costumbres de don Alonso Enríquez de Guzmán': les 'Epístolas familiares' d'Antonio de Guevara," *BH* 71 (1969), 174–90. In note 17, Redondo announces that he has discovered these plagiarisms.

13. See Francisco Márquez Villanueva, "Marco Aurelio y Faustina," *Insula* (Madrid), no. 305 (April, 1972), pp. 3–4. Márquez, in this very suggestive article, studies the relationship between the emperor and his wife and concludes that Faustina is the "axis" of Marcus's

life and that Marcus's sorrow at her death causes him to cease all literary activity—a conclusion at which the reader must arrive on the negative evidence that all of the letters appended to the work were written during Faustina's lifetime. Guevara creates the marital tensions out of a purely artistic will to investigate the unexplained complexity of the individuals "who," as Márquez puts it, "love each other in spite of mutual infidelities."

With regard to Faustina's "infidelity," however, it is well to remember that one of Guevara's favorite devices of characterization is to invert the traditional concept. If Marcus is the virtuous pagan *par excellence*, Guevara will show that he achieves this virtue in spite of his fleshly weaknesses. If Faustina is a byword for immorality (as in Boccaccio's *Concerning Famous Women*, chap. 96, by no means referred to "in vain" by anyone trying to penetrate Guevara's meaning), then Guevara will make her a victim of slander from the ex-mistress and even from her overexcited husband, but hardly an adulteress. The vilifications of Bohemia (that Faustina was not a virgin when Marcus married her and that she turns the palace into a brothel at night) are plainly to be taken as the excesses of hysterical jealousy, and must be understood in the context of extremes, e.g., p. 108, ". . . a daughter of his [Antigonus] was seen chatting and laughing with the Roman youths at the fountains, riverbanks, and public ovens—an infamous thing in Roman girls," and p. 129, "In those days, for a Roman girl to laugh with men was tantamount to a Greek woman's committing adultery with a priest." Any Roman woman who talked too much at festivities, spoke to a man without a chaperone, spent much time at her window, etc., "was forever considered infamous" (*ibid.*).

14. Classical historians frequently included letters as supporting documents or rhetorical ornaments for their works, much as Guevara himself does in the revised version of *The Golden Book*, where the letters appear scattered in the text. Spanish writers of the sentimental fiction and books of chivalry that Guevara deplores often incorporate exchanges of love letters in their stories. Guevara's decision to put the correspondence in a separate book takes advantage of this popular device for increasing the illusion of reality in a novel while at the same time renewing its power of suggestion. See Charles E. Kany, *The Beginnings of the Epistolary Novel in France, Italy, and Spain* (Berkeley, 1937). The University of California Publications in Modern Philology, vol. XXI (1937–1944). Kany notes the unusual place of the letters at the end of *The Golden Book* and suggests that it probably inspired a similar ending for *Euphues*. See pp. 61–64.

15. Márquez's article on "Fray Antonio de Guevara y la invención

de Cide Hamete," in *Fuentes literarias cervantinas*, contains a brilliant analysis of Guevara's novelistic techniques, much of which applies to *The Golden Book*, especially pp. 200–13.

Chapter Three

1. Lord North translated the title as *The Diall of Princes*, and I shall continue to refer to the work as the *Dial* for convenience. The Spanish title reads *Libro llamado RELOX DE PRINCIPES, en el qual va incorporado el muy famoso libro de Marco Aurelio; auctor del un libro y del otro es el muy reverendo padre fray Antonio de Guevara, predicador y coronista de su magestad y agora nuevamente electo en obispo de Guadix; el auctor avisa al lector que lea primero los prólogos si quiere entender los libros.*

Page references are to the folios of this edition, *r* standing for *recto*, "front," and *v* for *verso*, "back," of the numbered folio.

2. Sandoval (II, 47) reports that the emperor became ill with quartern fever toward the end of 1524, as a result of the siege of Pavia, the pope's indecision, and money troubles. His doctors advised him to leave Valladolid for Madrid, where he spent Christmas, 1524. Gibbs speculates that Guevara was with the court in 1524 and early 1525.

3. For a more circumstantial account of the "theft" of the manuscript, see the *Epístolas familiares*, part I, letter 42, p. 269 *ed. cit.*

4. Guevara, from 1529 on, favors the title *Marcus Aurelius*, though he had certainly named the first version *The Golden Book* or *The Golden Book of Marcus Aurelius*. Perhaps the work had already acquired a popular nickname, like *Celestina*, which appeared originally as *The Tragi-comedy of Calisto and Melibea*.

5. *Horologii Principum libri III* (Torgau, 1601).

6. Gilman, "The Sequel to 'El villano del Danubio.'" See note 9, chap. 2, above.

Chapter Four

1. *Aviso de privados ò despertador de cortesanos*, ed. A. Alvarez de la Villa (Paris: Sociedad de ediciones Louis-Michaud, n.d. [c. 1914]), pp. 48–49.

2. Joseph R. Jones, ed., *Una década de Césares* (Chapel Hill: University of North Carolina Press, 1966), pp. 61–67. All page references are to this edition.

Chapter Five

1. See note 1 of chapter four for the edition consulted. Page references are to this edition.

2. See Pauline M. Smith, *The Anti-Courtier Trend in Sixteenth Century French Literature* (Geneva: Librarie Droz, 1966), p. 32: ". . . it was probably the widespread success of the *Cortegiano* in Spain . . . which encouraged Guevara to write his *Aviso de Privados* for which there appears to have been no previous Spanish model. It would, however, be totally misleading to suggest that there was any indication, or indeed intention, of imitation of the *Cortegiano* on the part of Guevara in the work. The author's intention is rather to provide a guide for all those who wish to survive at court while at the same time preserving their integrity. Resigned to an abuse which he cannot eradicate Guevara attempts, in the *Aviso*, to come to terms with it. This declared intention is served initially by combative means and the opening chapters of the work contain an unexpectedly violent attack on court life and a dequisition [*sic*] on the ignoble motives of courtiers." See pp. 32–38.

3. Hayward Keniston, *Francisco de los Cobos, Secretary of the Emperor Charles V* (Pittsburgh: University of Pittsburgh Press, 1960).

Chapter Six

1. M. Martínez de Burgos, ed., *Menosprecio de corte y alabanza de aldea* (Madrid: Espasa-Calpe, 1952). Clásicos castellanos, 29. Edition prepared in 1914. Page references are to this edition.

2. For a different analysis and an illuminating study of stylistic traits, see Frida Weber de Kurlat, "El arte de Fray Antonio de Guevara en el *Menosprecio de corte y alabanza de aldea*," *Studia Iberica: Festschrift für Hans Flasche* (Bern and Munich: Franke Verlag, 1973), pp. 669–87. Mrs. Kurlat believes that Guevara originally intended to end the work with chapter 10.

3. *The Life of Solitude*, ed. Jacob Zeitlin (Urbana: University of Illinois Press, 1924).

4. Wilfred P. Mustard, ed. (Baltimore: The Johns Hopkins Press, 1928). Studies in the Renaissance Pastoral, no. 5. Smith, *The Anti-Courtier Trend*, pp. 22–24, adds greatly to the understanding of Piccolomini's sources.

5. "Fray Antonio de Guevara . . . ," pp. 352–53.

6. Gustavo Agrait, *El "Beatus ille" en la poesía lírica del siglo de oro* (Puerto Rico: Editorial Universitaria, 1971). Professor Agrait, the most recent scholar to study the antecedents and followers of the theme of the *vida retirada*, traces the fortune of the "two fundamental aspects of the theme—the dispraise of court and praise of the village" (53) from its period of "hibernation" (62) during the Middle Ages and its real point of departure in Spanish letters with the strophes

16–18 of Santillana's *Comedieta de Ponça* (c. 1436). Agrait considers Guevara's work of particular interest because it is the "culmination" of the criticism of chivalrous life-style steadily growing since the beginning of the fifteenth century. Following Isaza Calderón, Agrait notes that Guevara gives the theme a new aspect by adding religious considerations, expressed in terms of the opposition of city and village: the city is full of temptations, the village the ideal place to prepare the soul for eternity (80–83). He also notes the Senecan influence.

7. Smith, *The Anti-Courtier Trend*, p. 33: "All pretence of compromise [with court life], all hope of survival, is abandoned. . . . The work is an outright condemnation of courtiers and court life."

8. Smith, p. 34: "To criticise Guevara's descriptions of country life for their lack of realism and close observation, as some writers have done, shows therefore a complete failure to grasp the author's intention. The emphasis is clearly intended to be on the satire of court life, the praise of the rural life being chiefly a yardstick with which we are intended to assess the gulf between the ideal and the actual. . . ."

9. Dr. Smith sees this section as an intentional contrast with Castiglione, a contrast which made Guevara the "champion" of the anti-*Cortegiano* French authors of the later sixteenth century (pp. 36–37).

Chapter Seven

1. *Arte de marear*, R. O. Jones, ed. (University of Exeter, 1972). Exeter Hispanic Texts, II. The full Spanish title of the work is *Libro que trata de los inventores del arte de marear y de muchos trabajos que se pasan en las galeras.*

Chapter Eight

1. *Libro primero de las epístolas familiares*, ed. José María de Cossío (Madrid: Aldus, 1950–1952). 2 vols. Though the title does not indicate it, the second volume of this edition is the *Segunda parte*. A careful edition that identifies the addressees, explains historical references, and studies the problem of the dates is a desideratum.

2. I find it disappointing that Félix Herrero Salgado does not even mention Guevara in his excellent *Aportación bibliográfica a la oratoria sagrada española* (Madrid: CSIC, 1971); because of the immense numbers of editions of the *Letters* in all modern European languages and Latin, Guevara must surely be the most widely read Spanish preacher of all time.

3. Blüher, Karl Alfred. *Seneca in Spanien: Untersuchungen zur Geschichte der Seneca-Rezeption in Spanien vom 13 bis 17. Jahrhundert* (Munich: Francke Verlag, 1969), pp. 218–27 (subtitled "Seneca in moralischen Schrifttum: Antonio de Guevara").

4. Fidèle de Ros, "Guevara auteur ascétique," *Archivo iberoamericano* 6, nos. 22–23 (1946), 394–97.

5. *Las quatrocientas respuestas a otras tantas preguntas que el ... Almirante de Castilla y otras personas en diversas vezes embiaron a preguntar al autor ...* The balanced style of the prose introduction, the accusations of plagiarism, and even the impertinent tone are all notably Guevarian. See Christoph E. Schweitzer, "La parte de Albertinus, Escobar y Guevara en el *Zeitkürtzer*," *Archivo iberoamericano* 18 (Jan.–June, 1958), 217–23. This brief but valuable article suggests, among other things, that Guevara's correspondence may not be merely literary exercises, since there is some proof that Guevara's fellow-Franciscan Escobar and the ex-Jewish doctor Francisco López de Villalobos also exchanged letters similar in tone to the *Familiar Letters* with magnates like the Admiral of Castile.

6. "Cartas del bachiller Pedro de Rhua," *Epistolario español* (Madrid: Editorial Atlas, 1945), pp. 229–50. Biblioteca de Autores Españoles, vol. 13. Edition prepared in 1850.

7. *Ibid.*, p. 237, n. 1.

8. Cf. Florentino Zamora Lucas and Victor Hijes Cuevas, *El bachiller Pedro de Rúa* (Madrid: CSIC, 1957), p. 115.

9. For an interesting account (in English) of the Guevara-Rúa exchange, see Ernest Grey, "Pedro de Rhua's Critique of Antonio de Guevara," *Symposium* 21, no. 1 (1967), 29–37.

10. *Epístolas familiares*, I, 308: "el caballero Tirán," the Catalan form, usually written *Tirant*.

11. My explanation of Guevara's passion for "authority" is in opposition to the plausible and well-argued thesis of Francisco Márquez Villanueva, who believes that "Guevara is the first European author who writes with deliberate indifference to traditional literary theory, free of commitments of any sort and of demands which impose upon literature any finality alien to itself" (*Fuentes*, 192). "His art is pure play of wit and imagination" without didactic or "authentic moral goals" (*ibid.*). To be sure, he must disguise his purposes with classical erudition and moralizing, but he uses these elements with novel irony and burlesque humor and converts them into one of the "pillars" of his style.

Limitations of space make it impossible for me to give more than a sketchy summary of Márquez's valuable ideas, as they are developed in a number of essays. I should like, however, to offer the following observations on his theories:

(1) Guevara's writings are not as homogeneous as Márquez, perhaps inadvertently, suggests. They show a hesitating development from the *Libro áureo* (written as early as 1518 perhaps) to the *Letters* and the last pages of the *Monte Calvario*, and Guevara is frequently unsure in his taste, use of devices, and intentions. Nor was fray Antonio a clear-sighted artist, hundreds of years ahead of his time, whose unshakable conviction of his superiority explains his dismissal of Rúa's criticisms. The unfortunate alterations in the *Relox* are his response to adverse criticism, his desire to conform to more acceptable literary conventions, and his vacillating confidence in his own art.

(2) Guevara's modernity (i.e., his early use of special techniques of characterization, author intrusion, and particularly the perverse humor and irony which makes Márquez doubt Guevara's "seriousness" or his credibility among his contemporaries) is not nearly so apparent to the reader who must wade through the thousands of pages of antiquated prose as it is in the persuasively written articles of Professor Márquez. Perhaps it was not quite so apparent to contemporary readers, either. Considering the astounding number of editions and translations, one would think that more than one perceptive reader (Cervantes) would have attempted to imitate some of these original traits, since they imitated the more old-fashioned traits in considerable numbers in "moral" prose, sermons, and novels (e.g., the letters in Lyly's *Euphues*, the "manuscript" source of Elyot's *Governor*).

(3) Perhaps the *sentencia profunda y doctrina sana* which Professor Márquez systematically rejects (*Fuentes*, p. 198, for example) did in fact seem important to Guevara and did not seem so trivial to his contemporary readers. Such things as Wanckelius's laborious translation and "reconstruction" of the *Relox de príncipes* or the publication as late as 1760 of four hundred maxims from the works of Guevara suggest that the trite intellectual content—as opposed to artistic value —*did* matter.

Is it necessary to reject the old idea that Guevara was, by intention and result, a "moralist," or whatever one wants to call Guevara as counsellor, spiritual adviser, *filósofo* (as he uses the term), in order to reach a balanced appreciation of his work and his success? Is he, always and uniformly, free of "authentic moral goals" (*Fuentes*, 192)? I find it difficult to believe, without better evidence than Professor Márquez's intuition—which is very sound, usually—that "many contemporaries swallowed the hook of Guevarian pseudodidactism and attributed their pleasure in reading his works to their pious enthusiasm for the moral wisdom of the ancients" (*Fuentes*, 256). There are great stretches of the *Relox* where they would have had difficulty in finding anything else! Indeed, what is the difference, if one believes all that Guevara says in his windy prologues and "swallows" the didacticism, which does after all comprise, I should say, about 80 percent of Guevara's writings?

I am not convinced that a serious intent to inculcate traditional Christian and quasi-Stoic precepts for living is incompatible with fictionalizing, falsifying, "degrading" descriptions, or self-caricatures. The sermon manuals cited by Márquez (*Espiritualidad*, p. 50, n. 27) prove that humor and satire were common enough in the pulpit to cause the writers of the manuals to censure them as a usual practice. Surely that is not proof that all satirical preachers are not really interested in morals. Why should the exploration—not exactly evolution, since Guevara sometimes regresses, as does Cervantes—of such techniques as self-depiction in satirical terms not be viewed as another way to lure the reader to the morality of the work? What Rúa, Bayle, Ros, María Rosa Lida, and other excellent scholars have hated in Guevara is the falsification. They cannot see the remarkable technical advances of Guevara's works, especially in the *Libro áureo* and certain letters, because of their annoyance at his flagrant dishonesty. It is Márquez's great contribution to have seen clearly how Guevara uses falsification constructively.

Chapter Nine

1. Juan Bautista Gomis, ed., *Místicos franciscanos españoles*, vol. II (Madrid: Editorial Católica, 1948). Page references are to this edition.

2. Francisco Márquez Villanueva, "Fray Antonio de Guevara o la ascética novelada," *Espiritualidad y literatura en el siglo XVI* (Madrid-Barcelona: Alfaguara, 1968), pp. 30–31, n. 14, says that *oratorio* means "model monastery" in this context.

3. Cf. Márquez, *Espiritualidad*, p. 49, n. 26 on Guevara's "dire" influence on preaching: "Guevara should be considered therefore as the real father . . . of *gerundianismo.*"

4. "Guevara, auteur ascétique," pp. 339–404.

5. Fr. Ros doubts this. See p. 369, note 43.

6. I have used the Antwerp, 1550, ed. of both parts.

7. Márquez has very astutely observed one probable allusion to Charles V's attempts to get money from the church and nobility. See *Espiritualidad*, p. 33, n. 18.

8. Cf. the borrowings of a famous Franciscan saint: St. Bernardino of Siena, an immensely famous fifteenth-century preacher, translated

hundreds of his sermons into Latin, as a collection of models for preachers, arranged in series. "Much of the material for these sermons is taken from previous writers, and generally without acknowledgment. Bernardino had no hesitation in drawing on the writings of others. His sole desire was to teach and convince his audiences, and if some scholar had written passages which he thought suitable for his purposes, he gladly employed them. A good deal is here taken from Duns Scotus and from Alexander of Hales, but perhaps most from Ubertino of Casale, whose *Arbor Vitae Crucifixae* was ransacked. Bernardino never refers to Ubertino by name; but of the 101 chapters of the *Arbor*, he has used forty-seven, sometimes copied down almost word for word." John Moorman, *A History of the Franciscan Order from its origins to the year 1517* (Oxford, 1968), p. 460.

9. Márquez's essay contains at least one conclusion which is, it seems to me, unwarranted. In the division entitled "The Passion according to Guevara," pp. 38–47, Márquez attempts to persuade the reader that Guevara turns the death of Jesus into a tawdry, morbid, anachronistic, and weirdly funny vision which approaches "pure fiction" (44). Even if the reader grants this, however, is he *therefore* forced to conclude (p. 46) that "*The Mount of Calvary* and indeed all of the religious writing of Guevara was not, in fact, taken very seriously, as we know occurred with their author. In reality, it was not read as edifying matter but as a piece of entertainment literature, like the other works of Guevara, from which it differs only in its slight thematic framework" (46)? The success of *The Mount of Calvary* in translation, where the striking anachronisms and "hispanization" were attenuated (cf. p. 53) and where puns and suggestive association of words are lost altogether, would seem to contradict such a conclusion.

Selected Bibliography

PRIMARY SOURCES

The best list of editions of Guevara's publications is that of Lino G. Canedo (See Secondary Sources). Canedo's work has been supplemented and corrected by subsequent bibliographies (see Babilas, Gibbs, Mancini, Schweitzer, and Smith in Secondary Sources). I have indicated in each chapter which text I used as a basis for my study and translations, but for the reader's convenience, I shall repeat them here:

Arte de marear. Edited by R. O. Jones. Exeter: Exeter University Printing Unit, 1972. Exeter Hispanic Texts, II.

Aviso de privados ò despertador de cortesanos. Edited by A. Alvarez de la Villa. Paris: Sociedad de ediciones Louis-Michaud, n.d. [c. 1914].

Libro áureo de Marco Aurelio. Edited by R. Foulché-Delbosc. *Revue Hispanique* 76, no. 169 (1929), 6–319.

Libro primero de las epístolas familiares. Edited by José María de Cossío. Madrid: Aldus, 1950–1952. Two vols., the second of which is actually *Segunda parte de las epístolas familiares*.

Menosprecio de corte y alabanza de aldea. Edited by M. Martínez de Burgos. Madrid: Espasa-Calpe, 1952 [reprint of 1914 ed.]. Clásicos castellanos, 29.

Monte Calvario. Antwerp: Martin Nucio, 1550.

Oratorio de religiosos y ejercicio de virtuosos. Edited by Juan Bautista Gomis. In *Místicos franciscanos españoles*, vol. II. Madrid: Editorial Católica, 1948.

Segunda parte del libro llamado Monte Calvario. Antwerp: Martín Nucio, 1550.

Una década de Césares. Edited by Joseph R. Jones. Chapel Hill: University of North Carolina Press, 1966.

SECONDARY SOURCES

This selected bibliography contains books and articles on Guevara and works which devote special attention to Guevara. It omits articles which are principally biographical or bibliographical unless they have appeared since the publication of the biography of Gibbs (1960) or the bibliography of Canedo (1946) or are unusually valuable. It also omits theses and dissertations if they appear in published form at a later date, works on the controversy over Guevara and euphuism (because Grey covers that area thoroughly), and reviews, as well as articles that are too elementary.

Since the publication of Canedo's bibliography there have been new editions of the following works.

1. New Editions

Oratorio de religiosos. Edited by Fr. Juan Bautista Gomis in *Místicos franciscanos españoles.* Madrid: Editorial Católica 1948. II, 449–750.

Libro primero [y segundo] de las epístolas familiares. Edited by José María Cossío. Madrid: Aldus, 1950–52. 2 vols.

El libro áureo del emperador Marco Aurelio con el Reloj de príncipes. Edited by Juana Granados. Milan: "La Goliardica"-Edizioni Universitarie, n.d. [1953?]. Typewritten selections, apparently prepared for classes at the Università Commerciale Luigi Bocconi.

Una década de Césares. Edited by Joseph R. Jones. Chapel Hill: University of North Carolina Press, 1966. Useful introduction and bibliography.

The diall of Princes (London, 1557). The English Experience, Facsimile no. 50. Amsterdam: Theatrum Orbis Terrarum; NY: Da Capo Press, 1968.

Epístolas familiares. Edited by William Rosenthal. Zaragoza: Editorial Ebro, 1969. An abridged student edition, full of errors.

Menosprecio de corte. Zaragoza: Editorial Ebro, 1969 (?). I have not seen this edition.

Arte de marear. Edited by R. O. Jones. Exeter: Exeter University Printing Unit, 1972.

2. Scholarly Books and Articles

In order to shorten the entries, I have used normal American abbreviations for titles of journals, as found in Publications of the Modern Language Association. They are

BH, Bulletin Hispanique
MLN, Modern Language Notes
MLR, Modern Language Review
N & Q, Notes and Queries
Neophil, Neophilologus

NRFH, Nueva Revista de Filología Hispánica
REH, Revista de Estudios Hispánicos
RFE, Revista de Filología Española
RHL, Revue d'Histoire Littéraire de la France
RHM, Revista Hispánica Moderna
RJ, Romanistiches Jahrbuch
RLC, Revue de Littérature Comparée
RLR, Revue des Langues Romanes
RomN, Romance Notes
SP, Studies in Philology

AGRAIT, GUSTAVO. *El "Beatus ille" en la poesía lírica del Siglo de Oro*. Mexico City: Editorial Libros de México, 1971. Published by Editorial Universitaria of the University of Puerto Rico. Pp. 82–85.

BABILAS, LYDIA ANTONIO. *Antonio de Guevara und sein Uebersetzer Cosimo Baroncelli: Ein Stilvergleich*. Ph.D. Diss. Munchen Universität, 1963.

BLÜHER, KARL ALFRED. *Seneca in Spanien*. Munich: Francke Verlag, 1969. Pp. 218–28 ("Seneca im moralischen Schrifttum: Antonio de Guevara").

CAMPRUBI, MICHEL. "Le style de Fray Antonia de Guevara à travers les *Epístolas familiares*." *Caravelle* 11 (1968), 131–50.

CANEDO, LINO G. "Fray Antonio de Guevara, Obispo de Mondoñedo." *Archivo ibero-americano* 6, nos. 22–23 (1946), 283–330.

—————. "Las obras de Fray Antonio de Guevara: Ensayo de un catálogo completo de sus ediciones." *Archivo ibero-americano* 6, nos. 22–23 (1946), 441–603.

CASTRO, AMÉRICO. "Antonio de Guevara. Un hombre y un estilo del siglo XVI." *Boletín del Instituto Caro y Cuervo* I (1945), 46–67. Translated and used as the "Introductory Essay" of the pamphlet *Antonio de Guevara: El villano del Danubio y otros fragmentos* (Princeton: Princeton University Press, 1945). Reprinted in *Semblanzas y estudios españoles* (Princeton: Princeton University Press, 1956), pp. 53–73. Reprinted in *Hacia Cervantes*, 3rd ed. Madrid: Taurus, 1967. Pp. 86–110. Pp. 110–17 is Castro's answer to Spitzer.

CLAVERÍA, CARLOS. "Más sobre Guevara en Suecia." *RFE* 28 (1944), 83–85.

CLÉMENT, LOUIS. "Antoine de Guevara: ses lecteurs et ses imitateurs français au XVIᵉ siècle." *RHL* 7 (1900), 591–602, and 8 (1901), 214–33.

CORREA CALDERÓN, E. "Guevara y su invectiva contra el mundo."
    Escorial 12 (July, 1943), 41–68.
COSTES, RENÉ. *Antonio de Guevara: Sa Vie.* Paris: E. de Boccard;
    Bordeaux: Feret, 1925. Bibliothèque de l'École des Hautes
    Études Hispaniques, Fascicule X, 1. First appeared in *BH* 25
    (1923), 305–60, and 26 (1924), 193–208.
————. *Antonio de Guevara: Son Oeuvre.* Paris-Bordeaux, etc., 1925.
    Fascicule X, 2.
DE ROS, FIDÈLE. "Guevara, auteur ascétique." *Archivo iberoamericano*
    6, nos. 22–23 (1946), 339–404. Reprint of an article in *Études
    franciscaines* 50 (1938), 306–32 and 609–36.
DÍAZ-PLAJA, GUILLERMO. *Introducción al estudio del Romanticismo
    español.* Buenos Aires: Espasa-Calpe 1953. Colección Austral,
    1147. Pp. 117–40 discuss "El hombre natural," with attention to
    the *villano del Danubio.* Originally published in 1936.
DUVIOLS, MARCEL. "Un reportage au XVIᵉ siècle: La cour de Charles-
    Quint vue par Guevara." *Hommage à Ernest Martinenche:
    Études hispaniques et américaines.* Paris: Editions d'Artrey
    [1939?]. Pp. 242–47.
ESCRIBANO, F. S. "Sobre el posible origen de la frase *il faut cultiver
    nôtre jardin* de *Candide* (con un apéndice de las obras españolas
    en la biblioteca de Voltaire)." *Hispanófila,* no. 22 (Sept., 1964),
    pp. 15–26.
ESPINER, JANET GIRVAN. "Quelques érudits français du XVIᵉ siècle et
    l'Espagne." *RLC* 20 (1940–1946), 203–309.
FELLHEIMER, JEANNETTE. "Hellowes' and Fenton's Translations of
    Guevara's *Epístolas familiares.*" *SP* 44 (1947), 140–56.
FLECNIAKOSKA, JEAN-LOUIS. "Une épître d'Antonio de Guevara et
    la *Loa entre un cortesano y un villano.*" *RLR* 75 (1962), 1–13.
GARCÍA DE LA FUENTE, A. "Los Fueros de Badajoz publicados por
    Fray Antonio de Guevara, obispo de Mondoñedo." *Revista del
    Centro de Estudios Extremeños* 5 (1931), 195–208.
GEORGE, THOMAS. "Samuel Rowland's 'The Betraying of Christ' and
    Guevara's 'The Mount of Calvarie': An example of Elizabethan
    plagiarism." *N & Q,* no. 212 (Dec. 1967), pp. 467–74.
GIBBS, J. *The Life and Prose Style of Fray Antonio de Guevara.* Ph.D.
    Diss. Oxford University, 1951. I could not consult Gibbs's val-
    uable dissertation until after this book was in proof, so I can
    give only the briefest account of its contents. I found the
    following portions to be most useful: Ch. 3, a bibliography of
    editions of the works of Guevara, 640 items, which supplements
    and corrects Canedo; pp. 97 ff., an analysis of Guevara's rhe-
    torical procedures, with tabulations for each work; Ch. 6, with

detailed tables, on "The Absorption of the *Libro Aureo* into the *Relox de Principes*"; Chs. 12–14, on Guevara's ornaments, prose-rhythms, and probable models; Ch. 17, *testimonia*; and Ch. 18, a summary of Gibbs's findings regarding all aspects of Guevara's style.

————. "Two additions to the Italian bibliography of Antonio de Guevara." *MLR* 43 (1948), 244–46.

GILMAN, STEPHEN. "The Sequel to 'El villano del Danubio.'" *RHM* 31 (1965), 174–84.

GÓMEZ-TABANERA, JOSÉ MANUEL. "*La plática del villano del Danubio*, de fray Antonio de Guevara, o las fuentes hispanas de la concepción europea del *Mito del Buen Salvaje*." *Revista Internacional de Sociología* 24 (1966), 297–316.

GREY, ERNEST. *Guevara, a Forgotten Renaissance Author.* The Hague: Martinus Nijhoff, 1973.

————. "Pedro de Rhua's critique of Antonio de Guevara." *Symposium* 21, no. 1 (Spring 1967), 29–36.

IIAMS, CARLTON L. *Aegidius Albertinus and Antonio de Guevara.* Ph.D. Diss. Berkeley, 1956. I have not seen this work.

ISAZA CALDERÓN, B. *El retorno a la naturaleza: Los orígenes del tema y sus direcciones fundamentales en la literatura española.* Madrid: Bolaños y Aguilar, 1934. Pp. 205–32.

JONES, JOSEPH R. "A Note on Antonio de Guevara and King James I." *RomN* 14, no. 1 (1972), 168–72.

————. "Allusions to Contemporary Matters in Guevara's *Década*." *RomN* 5, no. 2 (1964), 192–99.

————. "El contenido folklórico de las 'Constituciones sinodales' de 1541 del Obispo Guevara." *Revista de Dialectología y Tradiciones Populares* 25, nos. 1 and 2 (1969), 53–66.

————. "El doctor Hernando de Guevara, del Consejo de Su Majestad." In *El Cardenal Albornoz y el Colegio de España*. Bologna: Real Colegio de España, 1972. II, 295–307.

————. "Fragments of Antonio de Guevara's Lost Chronicle." *SP* 63, no. 1 (Jan., 1966), 30–50.

————. "Topoi of Dedication in the Prologues of Gracián's *Discreto* and Guevara's *Década*." *RomN* 7, no. 1 (1965), 54–57.

KARL, LOUIS. "Note sur la fortune des oeuvres d'Antonio de Guevara à l'étranger." *BH* 35 (Jan.–March, 1933), 32–50.

LIDA DE MALKIEL, MARÍA ROSA. "Fray Antonio de Guevara: Edad media y siglo de oro española." *Revista de filología hispánica* 7 (1945), 346–88.

LOPES, FERNANDO F. "Traduções portuguesas de Fray António de Guevara." *Archivo ibero-americano* 6, nos. 22–23 (1946), 605–607.

López-Saiz, José María. "Sobre el *Arte de marear*, de Fray Antonio de Guevara." *REH* 4 (1970), 125–34.

Marichal, Juan. "Sobre la originalidad renacentista en el estilo de Guevara." *NRFH* 9 (1955), 113–28. Reprinted in *La voluntad del estilo* (Barcelona: Seix-Barral, 1957), pp. 79–101; *La voluntad* . . . also reprinted with bibliographical changes (Madrid: Revista de Occidente, 1971).

Mancini Giancarlo, Guido. "Antonio de Guevara e i suoi traduttori italiani." *Annali* 16 (1949), 147–74. Publication of the Facoltà di Lettere e Filosofia della Università di Cagliari.

Maravall, José Antonio. *Carlos V y el pensamiento político del Renacimiento*. Madrid: Instituto de Estudios Políticos, 1960. See pp. 183–205 and elsewhere.

Márquez Villanueva, Francisco. *Espiritualidad y literatura en el siglo XVI*. Madrid-Barcelona: Alfaguara, 1968. Pp. 17–66 ("Fray Antonio de Guevara o la ascética novelada").

––––––. *Fuentes literarias cervantinas*. Madrid: Gredos, 1973. Biblioteca Románica Hispánica, 199. Pp. 183–257. ("Fray Antonio de Guevara y la invención de Cide Hamete").

––––––. "Marco Aurelio y Faustina." *Insula*, no. 305 (1973), pp. 3–4.

Menéndez Pelayo, Marcelino. *Orígenes de la novela*. 2nd ed. Madrid: CSIC, 1962. II, 109–27. Originally published in 1905, this work has been reprinted numerous times. The edition cited forms vols. 13–16 of the *Edición Nacional de las Obras Completas de Menéndez Pelayo*.

Menéndez Pidal, Ramón. "El lenguaje del siglo XVI." *La lengua de Cristóbal Colón*. 3rd ed. Buenos Aires-Mexico: Espasa-Calpe, 1947. Pp. 65–68. Reprint of a 1933 article.

––––––. "Fray Antonio de Guevara y la idea imperial de Carlos V." *Archivo ibero-americano* 6, nos. 22–23 (1946), 331–38. An elaboration of aspects of his article "Idea imperial de Carlos V," which was published twice in Cuba, in 1937 and 1938, and re-reprinted in *Miscelánea histórica–literaria* (Buenos Aires-Mexico: Espasa-Calpe, 1943), 11–36. Colección Austral, 172. "Fray Antonio de Guevara y la idea imperial de Carlos V" has also been reprinted in *Miscelánea histórico–literaria* (Buenos Aires-Mexico: Espasa-Calpe, 1952), pp. 139–45. Colección Austral, 1110.

Mérimée, Paul. "Guevara, Santa Cruz et le 'razonamiento de Villabràjima.' " In *Hommage à Ernest Martinenche: Études hispaniques et américaines*. Paris: Editions d'Artrey [1939?]. Pp. 466–76.

MICHAUD, G. L. "The Spanish sources of certain sixteenth century French writers." *MLN* 43 (1928), 157–63.

MOREL-FATIO, ALFRED. *Historiographie de Charles-Quint.* Paris: H. Champion, 1913. Pp. 22–41.

MÜLLER, AGNES MARIA. *Das Ethos der Guldenen Sendschrieben von Antonio de Guevara*, Ph.D. Diss. University of Fribourg, 1930.

NORDEN, EDUARD. *Die antike Kunstprosa, vom VI, Jahrhundert v. Chr. bis in die Zeit der Renaissance.* Leipzig, 1898. II, 788–96.

PÉREZ, JOSEPH. "Le 'Razonamiento' de Villabrágima." *BH* 67 (1965), 217–24.

QUIROGA SALCEDO, CÉSAR E. "Embustes e invenciones en el lenguaje de fray Antonio de Guevara: Ensayo de estilística lingüística." *Románica* I (1960), 175–91. Publication of the Instituto de Filología de la Universidad Nacional de La Plata.

REDONDO, AUGUSTIN. "Un conseiller de Charles-Quint, ancien boursier du Collège Espagnol Saint-Clément de Bologne: le docteur Fernando de Guevara (1485?–1546). In *El Cardenal Albornoz y el Colegio de España.* Bologna: Real Colegio de Espana, 1972. II, 277–93.

————. "Une source du *Libro de la vida y costumbres de don Alonso Enríquez de Guzmán*: Les *Epístolas familiares* d'Antonio de Guevara." *BH* 71 (1969), 174–90.

SCHWEITZER, CHRISTOPH E. "Antonio de Guevara in Deutschland: Eine kritische Bibliographie." *RJ* 11 (1960), 328–75.

————. "La parte de Albertinus, Escobar y Guevara en el 'Zeit-kürtzer.'" *Archivo ibero-americano* 19 (Jan.–June 1958), 217–23.

SMITH, PAULINE M. *The Anti-Courtier Trend in Sixteenth Century French Literature.* Geneva: Librarie Droz, 1966. Pp. 32–38 and numerous other references.

SPITZER, LEO. "Sobre las ideas de Américo Castro a propósito de *El villano del Danubio* de Antonio de Guevara." *Boletín del Instituto Caro y Cuervo* 6 (1950), 1–14.

TURNER, PHILIP A. "Antonio de Guevara, *Libro áureo de Marco Aurelio*, Valencia, 1528." *NRFH* 4 (1950), 276–81. A description of a unique copy in Harvard library; suitably revised for *HLB* 5 (1951), 63–76.

URIBE, ANGEL. "Guevara, inquisidor del Santo Oficio." *Archivo ibero-americano* 6, nos. 22–23 (1946), 185–282.

VEGA DE LA HOZ, BARÓN DE LA, and the MARQUÉS DE LAURENCÍN. "La patria del obispo de Mondoñedo, Fray Antonio de Guevara." *Boletín de la Real Academia de la Historia* 65 (1914), 118–30.

WEBER DE KURLAT, FRIDA. "El arte de Fray Antonio de Guevara en el *Menosprecio de corte y alabanza de aldea*." In *Studia Iberica:*

Festschrift Flasche. Bern and Munich: Francke Verlag, 1973. Pp. 669–87.

WEYDT, GÜNTER. " 'Adjeu Welt': Weltklage und Lebensrückblick bei Guevara, Albertinus, Grimmelshausen." *Neophil* 46 (1962), 105–25.

ZAMORA, FLORENTINO. "El Bachiller Pedro de Rúa, censor de Guevara." *Archivo ibero-americano* 6, nos. 22–23 (1946), 405–40.

ZAMORA LUCAS, FLORENTINO and VÍCTOR HIJES CUEVAS. *El bachiller Pedro de Rúa, humanista y crítico.* Madrid: CSIC, 1957. Pp. 43–91. "Fray Antonio de Guevara, obispo de Mondoñedo, juicios críticos sobre sus obras," has a list of references by other authors to Guevara. This work incorporates the article of Zamora Lucas listed above in the special issue of *Archivo ibero-americano.* Curiously, the works ascribed to Rúa by Menéndez Pelayo in his *Biblioteca de traductores españoles* are not mentioned.

Index

173